VAULTING AMBITION

ACKNOWLEDGEMENTS

I would like to thank all the good people who so generously supplied me with the information which made this book possible. The roll call is long but necessary: Munair Zacca, Peter Ashbourne, Hilary Nicholson, Jean Small, Honor Ford Smith, Grace McGhie Brown, Barbara McCalla, Sam Walters, Ruth Ho Shing, Oliver Samuels, Basil Dawkins, Trevor Nairne, Pat Cumper, Louis Marriott, Alwyn Scott, Hugh King, Kwame Dawes, Mervyn Morris, Eugene Williams…

Dedicated to Kathleen and Claude Clarke for their endurance

YVONNE BREWSTER

VAULTING AMBITION
JAMAICA'S BARN THEATRE

It is unsuitable always to play in one style,
for not all men have the same character.
They are as varied in nature
as they are in their bodily composition.[1]

PEEPAL TREE

First published in Great Britain in 2017
Peepal Tree Press Ltd
17 King's Avenue
Leeds LS6 1QS
England

© 2017 Yvonne Brewster

ISBN13: 9781845233600

Supported using public funding by
ARTS COUNCIL
ENGLAND

CONTENTS

Kwame Dawes: Introduction 7

Chapter One: The Narrative 13

Chapter Two: In the Beginning 16

Chapter Three: The Name of the Game 28

Chapter Four: The Expanding Role of The Barn 43

Chapter Five: The Nineteen-Seventies 52

Chapter Six: Trevor Dave Rhone 60

Chapter Seven: Munair's Barn, 1974-1977 75

Chapter Eight: Behind the Scenes 82

Chapter Nine: Trevor Nairne at the Barn, 1979-1992 85

Chapter Ten: The Women 93

Chapter Eleven: Gracing the Barn 100

Chapter Twelve: Collaborations, New Partnerships, New Directions 105

Chapter Thirteen: Directors 109

Chapter Fourteen: The Prolific Basil Dawkins 115

Chapter Fifteen: Apres Nairne, the Beginning of the End 121

Chapter Sixteen: Postmortem 126

Appendix One 131

Appendix Two 134

Appendix Three 141

Index 143

INTRODUCTION

KWAME DAWES

The danger of declaring "first times" after a few decades have passed is that one could be wrong. That said, I can safely say that I was neither old enough or present enough to have been at the first productions at The Barn Theatre in the late 1960s. I was in Ghana. I was witnessing the unfolding of another cultural awakening, and though I was still under ten years old, I was there at the School of African Studies watching with my siblings the theatrical experiments with traditional Ghanaian ritual and folklore led by Efua Sutherland. I can still rehearse the sound of the cowbell knocking out the rhythm, which I would later rediscover under the guise of Latin music – the clave. The dancers moved, cajoled and coaxed by a choreographer or director. It was exciting because we children were not specially invited guests, but just a clutch of roaming urchins who had marked the School of African Studies as one of a series of possible stops for our adventures which included the ape cage in the tiny zoo on campus, the campus bookstore, the student cafeteria, the small brook filled with tadpoles and frogs behind a line of houses, and, of course, this place where theatrical things seemed always to be happening.

Indeed, what Yvonne Brewster's splendid retelling of the making of The Barn Theatre does is capture this peculiar phenomenon of youthful ambition, creative optimism and rollicking intellectual excitement that characterized the spirit of post-colonials, especially those fired with the zeal of a people who were now being asked to imagine an independent self as distinct from a colonised self. The men and women who started The Barn were shaped by independence or the idea of it, in as much as they were shaped by the giddy youth culture of the sixties blossoming in London, where some were trained, or in Jamaica where ska, reggae, Rasta were coming together in a not always lucid mix to create a sense of possibility.

The Barn was a post-colonial enactment, whether or not it's founders sought to describe it as such. And by its improvisational impulse, its wrestling with western and European aesthetics encountering a Jamaican sensibility that was increasingly distinct, The Barn represented a splendid confluence of these forces. It was driven by ambition – artistic ambition and a genuine desire to find a way to make a professional living in theatre in Jamaica at a time when few people could do so credibly. What is most striking about the early battles and discussions and passions in the coming together of The Barn was that there was a genuine fiscal sense of how to value art and how to create a theatre that was not amateurish. But it was one thing to conceive of a professional theatre in artistic terms, but to do so in fiscal terms was something else. At the time of the shaping of The Barn, there existed a model of artistic expression and performance in Jamaica, especially in theatre, that sought to elevate artistic professionalism while maintaining an amateurish economical base and ambition. People did theatre as a kind of hobby, though they did it seriously. Those who found a way to make a living in theatre were not embarked on a national project, and they, more often than not, left Jamaica quite quickly to try and make a living abroad. The Barn suffered because of this. In fact, as Yvonne Brewster's book demonstrates, there was a high price to pay for this kind of ambition, and that price was paid not merely by the scepticism of the public about the validity of this act of making a living in theatre, but even among the key players.

There is, in other words, something quite instructive about what Brewster reveals about the economics of the theatre. Matters of ownership, of fiscal responsibility, of management, and of artistic risk dogged the theatre for years. To this day, in Jamaica, the challenges of creating a theatre that is at once popular, and thus viable, and at the same time artistically ambitious and credible, remains a deeply complicated one. The advent of the Roots theatre movement and its offshoots in the producer-driven theatrical enterprises that exist in Jamaica today, indicates, perhaps, how much such an ambition as The Barn's was at some levels doomed to fail. Of course, one can argue that someone like Trevor Rhone managed to maintain a credible artistic integrity even as he produced popular and financially successful theatre (and film) throughout his career.

The first play I saw at The Barn was in fact a Trevor Rhone play, and a play that was not one of his more famous pieces. *The Game* (1989) completely entranced me. I left the theatre thinking that I had witnessed an extremely remarkable and robust theatre moment. The currency of the play had a great deal to do with it. The play suggested that the entire political enterprise of Jamaica was essentially a game that could be broken down into simple and laughable elements. It was, though, wholly depressing and one could not help but be disturbed by the accuracy of the analysis. At a time when I was walking around deeply angry with the very real, life-changing effects of political power and the vindictive and insidious nature of political control, *The Game* stoked something in me. It made sense that I was moved. But I can say, in retrospect, that it was The Barn, its physical peculiarity, that shook me completely. Simply put, everything was "onto" me. I can't put in any other way. The theatre was a small enough space that I could see every detail and I could hear the breaths, the gasps, the groans and even the rustle of garments as the actors sweated across the stage. This was a physical play and I felt I was been exercised physically because of my proximity to the action. Even when it was clear that the actors had fobbed a line or missed a cue, it was exciting to watch the slight twinkle in the eye, or look of admiration as one actor extricated another from worries. I was watching consummate actors, it is true, but I was so close to the action that I could allow, from a Brechtian indulgence, to focus on the artifice of the staging. I knew that I was watching a play, and yet I knew that I was being transported. I was willing to let that happen.

So it is not difficult for me to enjoy Brewster's description of the early productions, their immediacy and even their flawed nature. It has been fifty years since those days of hopeful and inventive excitement, and one imagines that time can dull memory and even passion, but Brewster writes with the perfect combination of irony and enthusiasm when she describes the conversations, the hilarious circumstances that would lead to her family leasing out an old garage to be employed in a largely impractical enterprise that would, ultimately, change Jamaican theatre for good. Put another way, reading her account today, I not only understand and even envy the optimism and excitement of their project, but I have the sense that I am drawn to capture in my own endeavours the fundamental principles that led to The Barn, principles that can be replicated today, and that have been replicated, again and again, by great arts endeavours the world over.

The Barn did not bring us an aesthetic or ideologically driven enterprise, except in the sense that The Barn emerged out of the same spirit that drove the movement towards Jamaican political independence from Britain – one of confidence, a desire for self-worth, and a desire to control one's own destiny. According to Brewster's telling, the evolution of the project into one that would seek, above anything else, to produce plays that were not just relevant to Jamaica, but that were essentially Jamaican was a gradual one. It is arguable whether this intention always drove the work of the project, or whether, instead, it became one of the important benefits of the pressure of necessity – audiences growing increasingly interested in seeing

Jamaican works on stage, and actors and directors and producers carrying an ambition to see a genuine Jamaican theatre in operation. The fact, though, is that, above anything else, the team that formed the early leaders of this movement were, first and foremost, lovers of the theatre. They loved Shakespeare as much as they loved Wole Soyinka. Practitioners of the theatre – actors, producers and directors – are often presented with more complex ways of demonstrating their ideologies, even beyond the actual scripts that are directed. Each of these players had been involved in theatre experiences in Jamaica that featured the work of the great western play-wrights, but that still, somehow, introduced production values, principles, ideologies and aesthetics that could be accurately described as post-colonial and wholly rooted in the Jamaican ethos. They would have seen and been involved with productions like Carroll Dawes' *Macbeth*, which employed elements of Jamaican folk life and the nuances of Jamaican social and political life in interpreting and, in many ways, transforming the work of Shakespeare. Thus, The Barn was a space in which artists could express the range of their creative selves, their education and their lived experience, but it would also come to be a space that celebrated the Caribbean playwright. Of all the playwrights whose work would be staged at The Barn, few could be said to have been more clearly the direct product of The Barn as was Trevor Rhone.

We should not be surprised that some of the great playwrights we have had throughout history can be associated with a single theatre space – a space that was open to experiment, innovation and risk. In the Caribbean, Derek Walcott is rightly associated with the Workshop Theatre of Trinidad. In Jamaica, Trevor Rhone's development will always be associated with The Barn Theatre. The Barn may not have had a repertory company, but it had a steady and consistent roster of actors and production support that assured Rhone of a space where he would always be able to stage his work in the early days of its development. For this, alone, The Barn has given a great deal to Jamaican and Caribbean theatre. Trevor Rhone remains, arguably, the most important playwright Jamaica has produced.

Indeed, and not surprisingly given the close, complicated friendship that Trevor Rhone and Yvonne Brewster enjoyed for almost sixty years, one has the sense when reading this book, that she is actually talking to Trevor Rhone, tossing out memories, interpretations of history, theatrical critiques, quarrels, and expressions of admiration and affection to him, as if expecting him to answer back. She is clear that in many ways the book is a dedicated to his memory, and yet, as makes complete sense, given how honest and unvarnished their long-standing working relationship and friendship was, the book does not ever lose track of its central goal of exploring how this small, innocuous space could be the laboratory for a massive and significant artistic endeavour that not only launched the careers of people like Trevor Rhone and herself, but that would always come to symbolize the complicated relationship that these artists had with each other, and, equally important, that they had with their country, Jamaica.

I remember doing a search of the *Daily Gleaner* archives a few years ago in an attempt to track down exactly when The Barn stopped being The Barn. I was also trying to find out what had become of the space. The steady movement towards dissolution was tracked, albeit imperfectly, by the newspapers through a series of brief stories, and a few interviews. At the end of the day, it was a matter of resources – The Barn simply could not continue to be a sustainable enterprise. But there was in some of the things that Brewster was saying, a sense that the spirit that began The Barn as a space for innovation and artistic renewal, had now been lost. The space was now merely a place where the business of theatre in Jamaica could be transacted – a business that had lost some of its artistic integrity. It strikes me as deeply unfortunate that The Barn has literally disappeared. I am sorry for this because I believe that given its importance as a site for so much that has been critical to Jamaican theatre, its disappearance as a physical space and the lack of physical evidence of its existence, constitutes something of a great loss. This book represents the singular monument of its existence and its importance.

I regard myself as a product of the spirit of The Barn theatre – the spirit that is born of people who, at some point, stop saying, "They should do this and they should do that", and arrive at the place of recognizing that "they" must become "we" or "I" and then discover the dangerous, delicious, and enlivening power of this recognition. Whether it has been the theatre companies I began in Jamaica in the 1980s, or the Calabash International Literary Festival, or the African Poetry Book Fund, or the South Carolina Poetry Initiative, or the many other endeavours I have been involved with over the years, I recognize that my envy of what was achieved, and what I learned had spurred these young people to create something dynamic and lasting, had been a great impetus for me and continues to be exactly the kind of inspiration that guides the work I do today.

Reading this book, however, I am also learning that for our institutions to truly move beyond the first bursts of revolution into projects that continue to replicate themselves and that continue to remain vital over multiple generations, we have to pay attention to both the successes and failures of those institutions that have been trailblazers for us. There is no doubt in my mind that Brewster, by naming her book as she does, understands the complicated impulses that started this project. She is being funny, too, in her way of flaunting boldly her willingness to invoke the "cursed" play, *Macbeth*, to describe a project that may have, at moments, seemed cursed, but that sought to do a great deal more than satisfy the self-serving ambitions of its founders. I would like to suggest that Brewster is asking us to consider ambition more closely. She helps to understand that there can be something quite altruistic and patriotic about ambition, the kind of ambition that must drive the artist to make greater art, to stretch the bounds of their abilities to find something remarkable and unexpected. This is, in many ways, the very "vaulting ambition" that she is alluding to. And, in the case of The Barn, it drove the people who began the movement to scale all kinds of obstacles to get to the other side. One may suggest that what awaits us at the end of a leap is a fall, but that would strike me as a pessimistic view. After all, a good landing ensures that the horse can move on to the next obstacle at full gallop.

Yet there is, no doubt, a less attractive side to this title, and Brewster understands that. The tension in this drama – the drama of the life and death of The Barn – often revolve around competing ambitions and visions, the hubris of personality, the mistrust that struggles with intense love and shared vision. It can be said that the decades of continued existence of The Barn were possible because, despite everything else that may have challenged its very continuation, ambition – a shared vision for what a professional Jamaican theatre could look like – was the real spur pricking their intent. I dare say that this ambition replicated itself in the lives of some of the many of the artists associated with The Barn and, in that sense, the ambition that started things has continued to thrive. But I have to say that at the end of the book, I, too, felt a sense of loss, a sense that what might have been, or even, what should have been, was thwarted by some of the very things that have thwarted ambition and creativity in Jamaica. Our governments should read this book, and they should make a solemn vow to not allow an institution of this nature to simply go away with a whimper.

Lincoln Nebraska, October 2016

CHAPTER ONE: THE NARRATIVE

This small book has been on the back burner for many years, during which time I have been constantly encouraged to record something of the history of The Barn Theatre which existed for forty years in Kingston Jamaica between 1966 and 2005.

Carolyn Allen, a theatre academic, wrote to me way back in 2007:

> ....Just a note to ask, is anyone undertaking the writing of a history of The Barn theatre? I've had a little bee in my bonnet for a few years now (even before closure) particularly about the variety of ways in which the stage has been transformed for various productions. That's how it started. Now of course it begs to be about the whole story at the centre of the growth of "popular" theatre.
>
> If the task is already underway, can I help?

Another less delicate shove came from Honor Ford Smith who accosted me loudly, very loudly, in the restaurant of the Young Vic theatre in London. To paraphrase her colourful exhortation she pointed out that if I didn't do it, it would never be done and I quote: "Trevor dead and you will be dead sooner or later... so get on with it, Miss Yvonne!" The polite London pre-theatre diners were all enthralled by this conversation conducted in the strongest, most vibrant of Jamaican accents.

When I finally embarked on this chronicle it was originally intended to be primarily a tribute to my colleague and friend, the late Trevor Rhone. He'd written to me:

> So, Mrs Brewster, my friend for close on fifty years – good years Brewster with a little turbulence in between. The turbulence, a punctuation sign, a mere comma – never a full stop and that's a blessing to be nurtured and cherished and kept in a safe place in our hearts –.[2]

A tribute it remains.

However, the research attempted in order to complete the work has thrown up so many and varied experiences of myriad Jamaican actors, directors, commentators, audience members and, of course, playwrights, many of whom are now established figures at home and abroad, that the remit of the book has widened considerably and acknowledges influences from outside Jamaica and the Caribbean.

In writing *Vaulting Ambition*, I sought out the memories of other people, some of whose vision resulted in the formation of this small theatre in 1966. In looking at the development of a number of dramatists whose work was essential to the success of the ideas presented in the space, it will examine the Jamaican trend of producer-playwright, which began at The Barn, and which is now the hallmark of a very high percentage of theatrical presentations in the island.

The social significance of our venue is examined in the light of what went on before the existence of The Barn Theatre, and The Barn's particular contribution is put in the context of some of the other venues currently available for theatrical presentation in the capital city of Jamaica, Kingston.

However, the ownership, professionalism, context and content of the theatrical presentations on offer in the post Barn era are not intended to be a significant aspect of this publication. That should remain for a writer more involved with current Jamaican theatre to analyse and comment on.

Generous space is given, however, to giving an account of the early years in an attempt to put the record straight, as far as has been possible, using the limited resources available. It may be readily accepted that "in plucking the fruit of memory one runs the risk of spoiling the bloom"[3]. In practice, many blooms were in danger of spoiling. I have tried, nevertheless, to encourage contributors to the practice and the ethics of The Barn to stir up their memories of those years, with varying degrees of success. As Jamaicans, it appears we do not, as a rule, place great significance on archiving, and memory is often an art of embellishment. It has been a labour of long love to extract some of the personal details, even with help from the newspaper archives. This task was made much more difficult because those archive files of The Barn which did exist were borrowed to provide information for Wycliffe Bennett's large book on Jamaican theatre[4] but unfortunately were never returned. It is thought that an overzealous helper may have thrown them out with the rubbish.

However, moments of more recent personal elation and encouragement, such as hearing Jeremy Corbyn, the leader of the Labour Party in the United Kingdom, recently[5] in conversation with Nigerian, Booker prizewinning author Ben Okri[6] at London's Royal Festival Hall, refer to the influence The Barn Theatre 77 had had on his early political and creative thinking when a member of the VSO (Voluntary Service Overseas) in Jamaica in the late 1960s. It was a moment to cherish and an inspiration to finish this book.

Much of the information in this volume has been the result of strenuous but often unsuccessful attempts to dredge up the facts from, in some cases, the fog of half a century. There were scores who I invited to contribute who shied away from recall; others who were too advanced in age to summon up the details from their vast but failing memory stores. Very few reactions compete, however, with the actor in her late 80s who, when told she had appeared in a play at The Barn in 1976, could only muster up a stifled cry: "You lie!"

Endnotes:

1. (Epigraph) From *A Mirror for Princes* by Persian writer Kaykavus ibn Iskandar ibn Qabus, 'Unsur al Ma'ali (circa 1021-1098).
2. Trevor Rhone in a letter to Yvonne Brewster.
3. Joseph Conrad, *The Arrow of Gold* (1919).
4. Wycliffe and Hazel Bennett, *The Jamaican Theatre: Highlights of the Performing Arts in the Twentieth Century* (Jamaica: UWI Press 2011).
5. July 15th 2016.
6. Ben Okri OBE (1959-) Nigerian poet and author. Winner of the 1991 Booker Prize for *The Famished Road*.

CHAPTER TWO: IN THE BEGINNING...

In 1965, a number of young Jamaicans, some of whom had been trained in Theatre Arts either in Britain or the United States of America, came together in an alliance cemented by a shared sense of the frustration they had experienced upon returning home from their studies. They had met with little welcome, indeed an almost tangible hostility from members of the existing theatre establishment and offered virtually no opportunity of putting their training to any real use. Led by Sydney Hibbert, the instigator of the idea, who had returned from theatre training in the USA, and including six others – Grace Lannaman, Pat Priestley, Billy Woung, Munair Zacca, Trevor Rhone and myself, this group called itself Theatre 77.

The name, Theatre 77, was significant as it encapsulated the primary aim and objective of the founding members: to establish a fully professional theatre company in Jamaica in twelve years: sixty-five plus twelve makes seventy-seven.

In the absence of any home-grown scripts which met with approval from the group, Theatre 77's introductory programme of work ended up as a double bill of two plays, *Zoo Story* by Edward Albee and *Miss Julie* by August Strindberg. Much deliberation went into the choice of these two short plays. Although written seventy years apart, one Swedish, written in 1888, and the other American, written in 1958, we confidently expected them to provide the Jamaican audience with an evening's entertainment that offered two interesting choices of food for thought. As both plays dealt in their different ways with the struggle between the haves and the have-nots, between the lower classes and those who they serve, and social inequality is examined so brutally by both playwrights, we felt sure that audiences would see the parallels with post-Independent Jamaican society, so the double bill would be a sure winner.

The casts for this double bill were drawn exclusively from the members of the company. (It had been mooted that Leonie Forbes Amiel, as a graduate of London's Royal Academy of Dramatic Art, might join the group, but somehow this never materialized.) Sydney Hibbert directed *Miss Julie*, in which Trevor Rhone, Pat Priestley, Munair Zacca and Yvonne Jones (Brewster) appeared. Trevor directed Sydney and Billy Woung in *Zoo Story*. Sets, props, costumes, lighting, sound effects were the joint responsibilities of these six members. Grace Lannaman, the seventh member, was the only original member of the group not to appear on stage in either play. She had for some reason been on the periphery of things from the word go and, to be honest, unfortunately played very little part in the beginning of the group, and none in its future life.

Theatre 77 had little or no money to pay for rehearsal spaces for the double bill, so we were forced to use my parents' veranda at 5 Oxford Road for this purpose, whispering the lines so as not to disturb my father whose study was close by.

Oxford Road was at that time a highly desirable address, almost leafy suburbs. Number 5 was a large, five-bedroom detached house encircled for the most part by a veranda, in grounds of at least an acre, sporting elaborate gardens, fully grown fruit trees and a tennis court. A long circular driveway led to a large wooden garage in which all the family cars were housed, suitably distanced from the veranda and far away at the rear of the property.

Also at the rear of the property, adjacent to the garage, stood three rooms which were home to the live-in staff.

In spite of the social relevance, as we saw it, of the double bill of *Miss Julie* and *Zoo Story* to Jamaican society, and some fine performances, this programme of work failed miserably, due to over-optimistic audience projections, inflated egos, and a complete absence of financial and logistic planning. To be fair, we were all to blame for the fiasco. The first performance, presented in the Old Dramatic Theatre building on the Mona Campus of the University College of the West Indies, played to four persons. Audience numbers fell after that.

No reviews appeared in the press. Nobody paid us any attention. Needless to say the run ended prematurely, leaving behind a colossal debt. Storage room had to be found for the four thousand, nine hundred and ninety-seven of the five thousand elaborate black and gold programmes which Sydney, as producer, had printed in anticipation of a great success.

In a post-production, late night company meeting of long knives and bitter recrimination, called by an irate Trevor, and conducted amongst the cars in the garage at 5 Oxford Road, Sydney's immediate resignation from Theatre 77 was demanded by Trevor on the grounds of gross mismanagement. Trevor had assumed the role of leader. Unfortunately, not everyone was prepared to go along with this development.

Trevor recalls this moments in *Bellas Gate Boy*:

A sotto voce female voice remarks –

– *Who does Mr Rhone think he is? Like he is still playing God.*
– *I don't have to put up with this.*
– *Then resign. Pen. Paper*[1]

Grace Lannaman, Pat Priestley and Billy Woung promptly tendered their resignations in support of Sydney. That left Munair, Trevor and myself on this sinking ship of theatrical endeavour. We were in what seemed to be a no-win situation: making the debt go away was one thing, a tangible hurdle, but facing up to the reality that the reputation of the fledgling company was less than nothing, was another thing altogether. A bitter pill to swallow by the rump of a once confident band of seven.

The debt was considerable, overwhelming. None of the remaining threesome had any money. Munair had just left school at Jamaica College and his parents, having envisioned a brighter future for him in the commercial retail family business downtown, than one messing round doing strange things on stage in a tumbledown old building, were not minded to help. Trevor and I were pauperised junior school teachers at Kingston College. There were those who advised us to call it a day whom we thanked but ignored.

We were not finished.

Nil desperandum.

There was, of course, a hiatus between the dramatic post-production meeting and the new spurt of energy and imagination needed to make the original idea work, or at least to re-group. The energies of the three of us sagged badly in this period. We nevertheless continued to plan our next production, which was intended to rescue our reputations and set the Jamaican stage aright, and alight, of course. One should remember that the three desperadoes were Munair, a seventeen year old school-leaver with no theatrical training whatsoever, Trevor Rhone and myself who has both graduated from Rose Bruford,[2] he in the early 1960s and me in 1959.

The matter of the debt, not drama, was uppermost in our minds; the enormous mound of useless programmes were a constant bulky reminder of the failure we had experienced. They ended up hidden in a dark corner of the garage, from which they mocked, silently. Unfortunately, I have been unable to trace even one of these relics which may have survived the "bonfire of the vanities" in which they were finally consumed. The financial debt, however, was a less physical presence, which could not be dissolved in flames.

Trevor tells the story in his one-man show, adapted for the stage from his autobiography, *Bellas Gate Boy*:

We did not know where to start. Who to turn to? But God is good and angels abound.
    Yvonne's mother, Mrs. Clarke, heard of our plight.

– *Bring me the books.*
She paid off our debts and was our benefactor for seven years.
    To cut costs, we rehearsed our next production on Yvonne's veranda, right next to her father's bedroom, so we had to leave out all the swear words and be very, very quiet,
    One night, a message from Mr. Clarke.
– *Go rehearse in the garage.*
We pushed the cars out...[3]

My father, Claude Clarke, regarded all this theatrical activity as little better than an unwelcome distraction from real life. He had in 1956, under duress, paid for my three year's study at Rose Bruford. He had been influenced by a photograph of polite young ladies practising archery which appeared in the brochure of the drama school, and was under the illusion that Rose Bruford College was in reality a finishing school. My mother, always the interface, smiled sweetly, reminding him that this institution had been recommended by the British Council representative in Kingston.

However, in 1965, my father simply could not continue to put up with

the constant loud whispering on the veranda, and badly concealed snigger-
ing outside his study bedroom, which seemed as if it would never end. He
was a generous man, but a studious one as well, and the noise affected his
concentration. His suggestion to "Go rehearse in the garage" came out of
sheer desperation for some peace and quiet. Little did he imagine that this
suggestion would very soon lose him the use of his garage, as what he called
the "theatrics" wasted no time in fully commandeering the emptied space.
My mother had kept the peace as best she could, between the dreamers
rehearsing on the veranda in penetrating stage whispers, and he who
preferred to study and read in the silence and privacy of his study.

Pushing three cars out of the garage every night to clear the space for
rehearsals, and then at the end pushing them back again, soon lost its
charm. I can't remember why we didn't just drive them in and out. Trevor
would remember, but is not here to ask. I expect we thought the noise of
three engines starting up, which would have been heard from the study,
might have had something to do with this.

However, one thing led to another. It soon became clear that the space
in which we were rehearsing was ideally fit for this purpose. It gave us
freedom. The floor was reasonably level and the total area of this large
garage was approximately 1000 square feet, although at the beginning we
had only half of this space at our disposal. Junk took up the rest. Still a
sizeable rehearsal room was at least better than a narrow veranda.

The play which we had been rehearsing in whispers on the veranda as
our next production was one of J.B. Priestley's "time" plays, *Time and
the Conways* (1937). It was a very proper English play, which we thought
the Jamaican theatre-going public, which in those days consisted mostly
of Embassy people, expatriates and a thin crust of Jamaicans educated
abroad, would be sure to patronise. We secretly hoped to entice at least
some members of the elite Paul Methuen Garden Theatre audience
to see a Priestley play... More on the Garden theatre anon.

Work on the Priestley play progressed swiftly and happily, with the
new found freedom our rehearsal space offered. However, once we, the
three remaining members of Theatre 77, tasted the freedom and power
of having our own space, however basic, in which to experiment, the
notion of *Time and the Conways* became less and less attractive. As the first
production of the beaten but unbowed, slimmed-down Theatre 77, this
play was not really challenging culturally, nor did it sit comfortably with
our new confidence and ambition. Mr. Priestley's work was eventually
abandoned. The reality that we had no venue in which to present it to the

public suggests this decision might very well have been a face-saving ploy.

The question of what play to rehearse was a constant topic of conversation. Ideally, we would have liked to work with a new Jamaican script, but there were no contenders that passed our acid test. I often regret, in hindsight, that plays such as *The Creatures* by Cecily Waite-Smith,[4] for example, had not crossed our path; one can contemplate momentarily, from this distance in time, the arrogance of failing to consider, for example, the early Derek Walcott's *Sea at Dauphin!*[5] Finally Noel Vaz,[6] theatre pundit and director of the Creative Arts Centre of the University College of the West Indies, came to the rescue. He always kept up to date with goings on in British theatre and suggested Roger Milner's farce *How's the World Treating you?* (1967).[7] It begins with the arrival of a demobbed lieutenant at a transit camp minus his platoon and trousers. This had been enjoying a successful first run at the Arts Theatre in London and *was* reputedly quite political at that time.

We all respected Noel's opinion, so there we were.

Rehearsing is one thing, but mounting a full blown production is quite another. Especially with our lack of recognition and of funds – together with what were not so quietly regarded as our rather ridiculous aspirations to grandeur. The question of where it would be performed remained an uncomfortable niggle, hovering in the back of our consciousnesses.

It now seems strange that it took months for us to realise that the rehearsal space we had invented… created… could actually become our own small theatre: a venue in which to experiment with "our art". When this finally dawned on us, vaulting ambition took flight. We would turn our rehearsal room into our theatre. My mother (always the ally) had first to be convinced of the value of having her garage cleared, not only of years of family junk, but of the cars as well, so that the emptied space could be used as a small experimental theatre.

Even she took some persuasion over a number of months as to the wisdom of this endeavour. The question of public liability loomed large in her mind. Finally, after some heavy lobbying, she came on board, encouraging my father to recognise the opportunities this proposed change of use would provide: from garage to rehearsal room and swiftly from rehearsal room to theatre space, of having his cars exiled to the driveway, of having strangers at the rear of his house at all hours, parking their cars on his lawn, even asking for glasses of water, and on occasion to "borrow the phone".

No one mentioned where the exiled cars would find themselves. It was quite clear they *would* have to be parked in the driveway, but as soon as my mother had convinced her husband, the way was clear and the space was ours. Not only to rehearse in but to present plays to the public: a "found" space, a space free from restrictions, preconditions, a space exuding possibilities.

Before any of these exciting plans could become reality, the vast quantity of junk that had accumulated in the back of the garage over many decades had first to be cleared. This formidable task was made easier by the help of Mr. Drummond, husband of the housekeeper, who was one of the strongest, best looking men I had ever met. They said he was Cuban. There was, amongst other useless stuff, such as old car engines, an enormous cast-iron bath lurking in the back of the place. One evening, when Munair, Trevor and I were looking at it, wondering how on earth we would ever be able to move it, in came Mr. Drummond, who pushed us to one side with a loud hissing of his teeth, which spoke louder than words of derision would have done. He took the thing out. On his back. We never quite got over that.

Finishing the job of clearing out the place suddenly became a much more viable proposition. This was done with some hard labour, but in a relatively short time the ex-garage was ready to be used as an improper theatre, which would house our productions and remain our rehearsal space. We now had both our own theatre space and were debt free.

It might be useful here to mention, briefly, other venues which were available for theatrical productions in Kingston in 1965, in order to better appreciate the significance of the emergence of this small theatre space, The Barn.

There was **The Garden Theatre**.[8] Paul Methuen, an aristocratic, enthusiastic, generous, Scottish theatre addict, had turned the grounds of his impressive Kingston residence in Hope Road into The Garden Theatre, where, once a year, he presented a very successful and expertly produced season of Shakespearean plays. It was considered an achievement to get cast in one of these plays, or as the parlance went at the time, to be invited "… to join Paul in this year's season in the garden". Jamaican theatre royalty such as Louise Bennett,[9] Lois Kelly Barrow[10] and Leonie Forbes[11] were regular invitees. Others hoped and waited for the call while studying the iambic pentameter.

Then there was the **Ward Theatre**. This was the jewel in the Caribbean theatrical crown. It is an impressive early 20th Century proscenium-arched theatre building, seating just over nine hundred people. It had been built and decorated on the proven format of famous English theatre architect Frank Matcham, but designed in this rendition by Jamaican architect Rudolph Henriques, who had won the competition for the best design and had been awarded the handsome sum of nine thousand pounds sterling donated by Colonel C. J. Ward CMG, "as a gift to the people of Jamaica".[12] The new Ward Theatre opened its doors to a grateful Jamaican public in December 1912. The Ward was, however, large, very expensive to rent and did not lend itself willingly to the intimate, experimental often highly political work we were devoted to.

The Ward was also, at this time, the home of the annual Jamaican Pantomime, which initially had been almost truly a colonial outpost of British culture. In 1941, *Jack and the Beanstalk* was presented on its stage complete with principal boy in thigh-high boots. When *Jack and the Beanstalk* opened on Boxing Day in at 6.00pm, a black face on the boards was almost an oddity. Actually there were a token few: Winston White and members of the East Queen Street Young Men's Fraternal took part in the musical numbers, and Miss Ethlyn Rhodd, a school teacher, was invited to play the role of the witch.[13] The cast was, shall we say, very fair in complexion. The great success of Jack was followed by other English classics *Babes in the Woods* and *Aladdin* , *Cinderella* and *Beauty and the Beast*. It still had strong echoes of the British Christmas Pantomime. But by 1943 things had already begun to change, with the production of *Soliday and the Wicked Bird* in which Jamaican cultural references in the text foretold the destiny of the form.[14] The intervening seven decades have witnessed the progression from the principal boy, through the interpretations of the theatrical giants such as Louise Bennett and Ranny Williams[15] to the custodial reign of Barbara Gloudon.[16]

There was also **The Little Theatre** on Tom Redcam Drive, which seated six hundred. It had been built in 1961 and was then, and still is, the flagship of the Little Theatre Movement inaugurated by the English theatre aficionados, Henry and Greta Fowler,[17] who became leading figures in the Jamaican theatre, a couple of decades before in the 1940s. It was hired out at great cost for large-scale local productions, mainly Off-Broadway and West End of London hits. A committee of the great and the good managed the venue, which was relatively inaccessible to the likes of us for all sorts of reasons, including its suitability for work of an experimental nature. Nothing much has changed in half a century or more, although The Little Theatre is now the home for the National Dance Theatre Company of Jamaica.

Up on the Mona Campus of then University College of the West Indies, there was **The Old Dramatic Theatre**, the infamous site of Theatre 77's disastrous double bill, but not much used after this event. A number of non-faculty/student performances were given permission to be presented in one of the small lecture theatres. Lloyd Reckord[18] did memorable work there with his company, the National Theatre of Jamaica, and the now legendary satirical revue, *Eight O' Clock Jamaica Time*,[19] was presented there on numerous occasions.

The Centre for Creative Arts was built on campus in 1968. This housed two auditoria, one mid-sized, seating between 250 and 300, depending on configuration, and another smaller, more experimental performance space with stone seats figured in the round. These venues were used only occasionally for non-university shows.

Then there was of course Marina Omowale Maxwell's **Yard Theatre** located in the back yard of her home. This was the venue most in keeping with our ideas but it was used principally, and for a short time only, for Marina's work[20].

There were therefore few, if any, small independent theatres reasonably equipped and available for general use in Kingston during the mid-sixties. We set about creating one through necessity rather than prophetic vision. The idea and design was encouraged by both parents, my mother providing cash for the enterprise, and my father giving his professional help with the more technical aspects, such as the gradient of the auditorium floor in relation to the height of the proscenium arch and so on. George Carter, who was to prove an early supporter of The Barn, bless him, gave us an ancient lighting board. Others gave us a wide berth.

In subsequent years a number of small theatre venues, configured from large rooms in small hotels, and on occasion small rooms in large hotels, especially the Sheraton and the Pegasus in Kingston, played host to miniature theatre offerings.

Later, commercial buildings no longer in use, ex-cinema drive-ins and converted dwellings began to see a new light of day as small theatre venues, attracting attention and audiences. These were venues such as the Green Gables, The Little Little Theatre, once the lowly rehearsal space for the Little Theatre and now a theatre in its own right. Center Stage used the office facilities of a defunct drive-in cinema; The Pantry Playhouse Theatre Place came into being decades after The Barn had successfully led the way in providing local theatre for local people in an accessible venue. It appears that these venues have dealt more successfully with the changes in target audiences than The Barn, although as I write now, of these only Centre Stage, Green Gables and the Little Little Theatre appear to be still in the business of producing and presenting theatre.

The facilities in hotels such as the Way Out Theatre in the Pegasus have long ago disappeared. It is rumoured that Pablo Hoilett's[21] Theatre Place in Haining Road, Kingston no longer operates as a theatre venue.

Even more sadly the Pantry Playhouse, also in New Kingston, which bore the closest resemblance to The Barn, has joined this sad roll call. Established early in the 21st century by the cultured Karl Hart in the grounds of his family restaurant in New Kingston, it served up an eclectic entertaining and thought provoking menu of theatrical treats. However, in mid 2015 the shutters went up. The Jamaican on-line arts magazine *Tallawah* had this to say:

> The news of the Pantry's imminent closure is incredibly sobering to say the least, and harks back to the demise of The Barn Theatre, which still lingers in the hearts of many of its devotees. I like to think that were we living in more fiscally prosperous times, the theatre community would have been better able to assist the proprietors in keeping the doors open, rallying for a worthy cause.

Endnotes

1. Trevor Rhone, *Bellas Gate Boy* (Oxford: McMillan Education, 2008), p. 32. The reference to playing God stemmed from the often mentioned major role The Lawd God in *Green Pastures*. Trevor had played at Drama College in London.
2. Rose Bruford Training College of Speech and Drama (as it was then known) was founded in 1950 by Rose Elizabeth Bruford, drama teacher and harpist. Now one of Britain's foremost drama schools offering university-level professional vocational training for theatre and performance.
3. *Bellas Gate Boy*, p. 32

4. Cecily Waite-Smith (1910-1978) was a Canadian-born Jamaican who wrote such plays as *Sleepy Valley* (1952), *The Creatures* (1954), *African Slingshot* (1957), *Uncle Robert* (1958). She was one of the first playwrights to bring a sympathetic portrayal to Jamaican village life.

5. *The Sea at Dauphin* (Trinidad, UWI Extramural series, 1954, 1958).

6. Noel Vaz (1920-2009) directed for the Little Theatre Movement, worked with Louise Bennett on the pantomime *Bluebeard* (1948), directed Derek Walcott's *Drums and Colours* and taught at UWI Mona, retiring in 1980. See "Theatre Icon Remembered", jamaica-gleaner.com/20100118/ent4.html

7. Roger Milner (1925-2014) also wrote, *The Upper Crust* (1968), *My Family Came Over with the Normans* (1972), amongst other plays.

8. The Garden Theatre survives as the Louise Bennett Garden Theatre.

9. Louise Bennett (1919-2006), Miss Lou followed Claude McKay (*Constab Ballads,* 1912) in treating Jamaican patwa seriously as a vehicle for social commentary in verse. She was the author of many volumes of poetry from *Verses in Jamaican Dialect* (1942) to the very popular and influential *Jamaica Labrish* (1965). As well as her work on Jamaican pantomime, she was an immensely popular and much loved performer throughout the Caribbean, North America and the UK. For further insights see Mervyn Morris, *Miss Lou – Louise Bennett and Jamaican Culture* (Ian Randle, 2104).

10. Lois Kelly Barrow was a mainstay of the LTM and Jamaican pantomime. She was one of the co-authors of *Queenie's Daughter* with Louise Bennett.

11. Leonie Forbes (1937-) is known as Jamaica's first lady of theatre. She studied at RADA and worked for the BBC's Caribbean service, and on British TV, and thereafter in Jamaica from 1966 onwards. See "Leonie Forbes: Theatre's First Lady", www.jamaicaobserver.com/entertainment/leonie_forbes_103140_?profile=1463.

12. The Ward Theatre was declared a national monument in January 2000, but is now in a state of disrepair bordering on collapse. The problem is that the theatre is located in an impoverished area of downtown Kingston and its middle-class patrons are reluctant to visit.

13. Wycliffe & Hazel Bennett, *The Jamaican Theatre: Highlights of the Performing Arts in the Twentieth Century* (Jamaica: UWI Press, 2011).

14. This LTM pantomime was written by the poet Vera Bell, with a set by the distinguished Jamaican artist Albert Huie. It featured

Anancy as one of the villains that Soliday, the hero, successfully overcomes.

15. Ranny Williams (1912-1980) was a Jamaican comedian and playwright. He was the entertainment manager for Marcus Garvey at Edelweiss Park. He began as a performer of Amos 'n Andy blackface skits. Later he was part of a long-running radio show with Louise Bennett, *Lou and Ranny*. See *The Cambridge Guide to African and Caribbean Theatre* (Cambridge UP, 1994), p. 217. (Hereafter *The Cambridge Guide*)

16. Barbara Gloudon (1935-) wrote plays for the pantomime such as *Moonshine Anancy*. She worked in radio as a social commentator and talk-show host for RJR and published a book of patwa sketches, *Stella Seh*.

17. For more on this English couple, Greta Bourke Fowler and Henry Fowler, see Bennett & Bennett, *The Jamaican Theatre: Highlights...*, p. 271-275.

18. Lloyd Reckord (1935-2015) studied at Bristol Old Vic in the 1950s, returned to Jamaica in 1956. He established the National Theatre Trust in 1968, and produced over 40 plays in the next 20 years. He acted and directed, notably in his brother Barry's plays. He established a children's theatre. He wrote and performed his own one-man show, *Beyond the Blues*.

19. A satirical review by Tony Gambrill (1965) which played on the fact that for Jamaicans, 8 o'clock meant 8.30 – and then people were still late.

20. Marina ama omowale Maxwell is a Trinidadian poet, novelist and as a playwright author of *Play Mas'* (1968). She studied drama in London in the 1960s and was a prominent advocate for a decolonising Caribbean aesthetic. She lived in Jamaica in the 60s and 70s. Kamau Brathwaite was a prominent supporter and participant in her Yard Theatre movement. In his *The Theatrical into Theatre: A study of drama and theatre in the English Speaking Caribbean* (London: New Beacon, 1982, p. 85) Kole Omotoso suggests Marina Maxwell "practised her yard theatre format" at The Barn Theatre but no evidence that this was indeed the case has come to light.

21. Pablo Hoilett is a theatre, TV and radio producer, director and actor who worked in Jamaica, North America and the UK. He is perhaps best known for the JBC-TV comedic sitcom Lime Tree Lane (1988-1997). See *The Jamaican Theatre: Highlights...*, pp. 283-284.

CHAPTER THREE: THE NAME OF THE GAME

Why call our venture The Barn?

It looked a little like a Barn with the large wooden doors and the apex-shaped roof. It certainly smelt like one because of the dark brown, evil-smelling solignum woodstain preservative that Trevor insisted the place be treated with: hence The Barn. There are schools of thought on the matter of naming, one of which insists that the two Rose Bruford graduates (Trevor and myself) were paying tribute to the practice theatre in Sidcup, Kent, where they had both studied, called The Barn. I think not. Another was sure the name was a tribute to Garcia Lorca's famous experimental touring theatre company in Spain, La Barraca. There is no definitive way of telling where the name came from. Memory is unreliable, but there we are. I have been forced to come to terms with this fact during the writing of this study. However this is how the place was described in *The Gleaner*:

> Large and well ventilated, the building is made of aged pinewood with open rafters, and is painted with a dark, brown solignum. An unusual feature is the split-level stage. The barn effect will be heightened by the lighting which will be done with old buggy lamps.

There are murals by Megan Thomas, and all the work of the remodelling has been done by members of the company.

The entrance to the theatre is on Norwood Road, a cul-de-sac which will make it free from noise.

There will be ample parking-space for the seventy-five members of the audience who can be seated comfortably. They will have stack chairs at the start; but ultimately the company plans to have tiers of cushioned seats.

Clearly much of this copy was supplied by enthusiastic members of Theatre 77, and as often with these effusive situations the imagination ran a bit wild, especially in the matter of the seating. Claude Clarke had helped by determining the rake of the auditorium and had performed some professional checks on the sight lines and the seating capacity, but the theatre space had no chairs. I do not remember a split level stage. Nor does anyone else I have asked. The stage was actually at this time 22 ft wide and 19 ft deep with two entrances, one on the side and one in the central back wall. As there was no wing space, entrances and exits were physically demanding to say the least.

Hilary Nicholson, who came to live in Jamaica from the UK in August 1970, remembers:

> It feels as though The Barn was always on the edge, and sometimes in the middle, of my life. I have memories of dashing off stage into huge puddles, blinded in the darkness. We had to jump over stepping stones over muddy water when it rained. Memories of rats scuttling across the beams in the roof... but we loved The Barn, regardless! There was nowhere like it, the intimacy – I have memories also of working FOH (front of house) in that stifling box office, which also had an entrance onto the stage... So sometimes the divisions between FOH and stage crew and actors weren't that clear... no luxury of separate bathrooms for actors...

There had also been a venerable theatre cat, until it took to entering stage right and sauntering across the small stage mid-performance, at will. Hence the rats maybe!

Kay Osbourne,[1] one of the small number of women playwrights to have had her work, *Wipe That Smile*, produced at The Barn describes the place thus:

> The weathered wood construction, the old barn-wood windows, the low roof, the small size, the straightforward, end theatre layout, the close distance of the stage to the audience, and the blackness that engulfed

the theatre right before shows started enhanced audience anticipation and intimacy between the performers and audience.

Not only their garage captured from the Clarkes: theatre requires a lot of backstage support such as dressing rooms, prop store, scene dock, lighting and sound booths and so on. Soon the three small rooms built along one side of the garage, intended for use by the domestic staff, the washing lines, the coal pot[2] site were also commandeered to provide these necessities. We gave no thought to the consequences for the staff in our comparatively youthful arrogance.

Alwin Bully,[3] writing much later, describes the theatre like this:

Although it had its challenges – tight seating, poor sight-lines, low ceiling, almost no backstage, very basic dressing rooms – The Barn had a warmth and intimacy that gave audiences a most intense theatre experience that has never quite been replicated in other Jamaican spaces. It had the magical ability to draw people into the heart of a story and send them home dazed and transformed through having been there. I think that's what good theatre is all about.

The Guyanese man of theatre, Eugene Williams,[4] until his recent retirement, the highly regarded Principal of the School of Drama at the Edna Manley School of the Visual and Performing Arts, worked at The Barn on a number of occasions. He had this to say:

Given its location (proximity to public transportation), affordability for rental, intimacy and rustic ambience, The Barn Theatre became the most popular theatre space since the advent of semi-professional theatre in Jamaica, through to its demolition. I suspect that research would also show that since the seventies, with the emergence of the semi-professional and the mushrooming of commercial theatre, the capacity of the auditorium, dressing rooms and architecture of The Barn Theatre also provided some dramaturgical and business influence on the mainstream commercial offerings generally in Jamaica. Unlike the so called Roots productions which were mounted at the Ward Theatre and school halls, the Pantomime which utilised the Ward and the Little Theatre, as well as the non-commercial productions that were staged at the Creative Arts Centre UWI, The Barn attracted productions with smaller casts and limited locations that were primarily realistic with interior sets. The approximately 15 feet by 20 feet stage, framed by low rafters and vertical walls, beyond which there was hardly any conventional backstage, became the proscenium model for the emerging commercial stage and the platform for amazing creative choices from playwrights, directors and set designers. Had this space not emerged as a viable theatre facility through the generosity of the Clarke family in 1965, with replications such as Stage One (New Kingston), The Way Out Theatre (Pegasus) and several contemporary versions, the semi-professional/commercial theatre would probably have had an entirely different trajectory.

Theatre 77's major obstacle, lack of venue, now overcome, however lacking in finesse it may have been, our first production of a full-blown script, *How's the World Treating You?* needed to be cast. The printed script called for fourteen persons. I believe we managed with eight.

As often with emotional feuds, fences were mended with the properly indignant members of the original company, who had given us three a wide berth after their resignations. One happy outcome was that the cast of *How's the World Treating You?* included a pacified Sydney Hibbert, Billy Woung and Pat Priestley. They once again joined forces with Trevor Rhone, Munair Zacca and Yvonne Jones. (Grace Lannaman was also helping for a while but understandably did not fully regain her enthusiasm). Welcome additions to the cast were Pamela Hitchens (now Mordecai), Vin McKie who was a fellow teacher at the Kingston College Junior school at Melbourne, and Andrew Garbutt, both of whom were to become well known faces on The Barn stage. Directed by Trevor, this English farce was the first play produced in the history of The Barn Theatre. It turned out to be a generally successful production, well costumed with an impressive set and relatively large cast. It played to an audience which grew steadily from very few to fifty or so people per night. It had taken some time for these changes to come about from the end of the opening double bill in 1965 to July 1966 when the production of *How's the World ...* opened.

As one of many futile attempts to get some well needed publicity, company members were encouraged to write short paragraphs describing their individual careers for possible promotional use. Some did:

PAT PRIESTLEY has had considerable theatre experience, and played a variety of parts with the University Players while still an undergraduate at the University of the West Indies. She has also acted with many of the leading drama groups in Jamaica. She appeared in *Hamlet*, played Ismene in Racine's *Phedre* and Mrs. Shuttlewaite in T.S.Eliot's *The Cocktail Party*.

PAM HITCHENS[5] was seen recently in Kingston in *King Lear*. While completing a degree course at university of Boston, she gained considerable experience with the Drama Society there, and played "Alice" in the premier production of Gabriel Marcel's *La Chapelle Ardente*, in Newton,

Massachusetts. After returning home, she appeared in *The Bald Soprano*, Ionesco's controversial play, and *Mountain Lion* for which she won the Best Supporting Actress Award in the Jamaica Festival. More recently she was seen as Lavina in the *Cocktail Party*, and she also played in the *Purification*.

GRACE LANNAMAN studied drama at the New York University School of Dramatic Art, where she appeared in a number of plays including *Amphitryon 38*, *The Enchanted Cottages*, *The Remarkable Mr. Pennypacker* and *Angel Street*. Since returning to Jamaica she has taken part in *The Merchant of Venice*, *La Ronde*, *Miriamy*, *The Bald Soprano* and *Signarelle*.

YVONNE JONES [Brewster] trained at The Royal Academy of Music in London and Rose Bruford College, where she took part in plays such as *Spring 1600*, *Peer Gynt* and the *Caucasian Chalk Circle*. While in the United Kingdom she also appeared in repertory at the Colchester and Guildford Theatres. She was heard frequently on the B.B.C. in radio plays, and broadcasts. Among her own productions are two of Chekhov's one-act plays *The Bear* and *The Proposal*. She was also seen in the recent Little Theatre Movement's pantomime *Morgan's Dream of Old Port Royal* at the Ward Theatre, Kingston.

SYDNEY HIBBERT trained in London at both The Royal Academy of Dramatic Art and the Guildhall School of Music and Drama. He won two British Council Drama Awards and the Shakespeare Characterization Award. (He later completed graduate studies in Speech Communication and Theatre Arts at Illinois State University USA).

TREVOR RHONE trained at the Rose Bruford College of Speech and Drama from 1960 to 1963. He appeared on TV in *Z-Cars* and *Front Page Story* as well as in several documentary programmes. He played the Prince of Morocco in *The Merchant of Venice,* produced by the Greater London Theatre Company. He has appeared locally in two pantomimes, in productions by the Caribbean Thespians, and as Oberon in Little Theatre's Movement's *A Midsummer Night's Dream*.

Munair Zacca, wrote no blurb. Having only recently left secondary school at Jamaica College, never having done any previous work in theatre, there was actually nothing to write about. For some long forgotten reason neither did Billy Woung, nor Vin McKie or Andrew Garbutt, who were also members of the cast.

There was, at last, some interest shown by the press, or to be more precise in the *Daily Gleaner* which gave us some encouraging editorial. Just before *How's the World Treating* opened at The Barn, *The Gleaner* "society" column, Merry-go-round, of the 14th June 1966, devoted a relatively in-depth article on Theatre 77 in lieu of any serious review of the work. This mainly reproduced almost word for word the details of some of the acting company's curriculum vitae. The article did also comment on the wide ranging aspirations of the Theatre 77 company, and gave details of The Barn auditorium which are interesting and informative, half a century on:

> ...For the time being they will choose plays with small casts; later they will have artists making plays with small casts. They will also have artists making guest appearances, among whom they very much hope to be able to number Mike Maberling who is giving such an excellent performance as Mercutio in *Romeo and Juliet* at the moment. Easton Lee will be guest-producer and Sam Hillary and Dennis Scott have agreed to be associated with the company as writers.
>
> With such an impressive array of talent at their disposal, one would have thought that Theatre 77 would have appeared as a full-fledged company. But with commendable modesty they decided that they needed at least ten years of intense work together to establish a style and projection of their own. For visual effect and luck they added another year.
>
> Theatre 77 is consequently more than a name; it is a target. Through the generosity and kindness of Mr. and Mrs. Claude Clarke of 5 Oxford Road, the group began to use a large garage on the premises as a rehearsal studio. It will now be used as their theatre. They feel that the public will appreciate the "barn" atmosphere which they have given to it... Theatre 77 aims at experimenting in studio and workshop, with International Drama, in finding West Indian work, in intimate theatre, and by selection to build a full repertoire around this premises.
>
> The theatre-loving public will certainly wish them well.

Beyond the constant worry, the single overwhelming problem of this new theatre space was lack of seating, except on cushions on the floor of the auditorium. In spite of the lofty aims mentioned in the *Gleaner* article, there were no chairs: definitely no padded seating. The gradient of the auditorium to accommodate the seating had been worked out, but we had no money to buy chairs to complete the job. Trevor again, in *Bellas Gate Boy*:

> We had no money to buy or rent chairs. Quandary. 'Happening' was the buzz word at the time. We'd turn the opening into a Happening. 'Bring your own cushion.' Come opening night, the big question. Would anybody show up? 8.30 curtain. 8.15, nobody. Cars kept coming down the road. Coming down the road. Five people with cushions...' (p. 34)

More people on stage than in the audience, but at least one more than for the ill-fated double bill. Happily, audiences grew. It even became an in-thing to arrive with the largest most colourful cushion each member of the uptown in-crowd could find. I have a personal memory of the late lamented uncrowned queen of the Jamaican Pantomime, its executive director, Greta Fowler, who was a large white woman generously supplied with cleavage, and her husband, the lovely Henry Fowler (to both of whom the Jamaican Pantomime owes an incredible debt of gratitude) arriving chauffeur-driven one evening, cushions in hand, having great difficulty actually getting down low enough to sit on the concrete floor. One sharp wit in the audience said sotto voce, "Unnu see what jungle claat come to?" Greta's dresses were always affairs of many yards of African print, but I digress. That the Fowlers found the concept of bringing one's own cushion "charming and amusing" was welcomed by us, because where the Fowlers led, the wannabe disciples followed. Our audience numbers were quite reasonable as a result.

The important thing was that with the growth of the audiences, some quietly confident reassessment of what sort of theatre product to aim for could now be cautiously contemplated, or even, at a push, put to the test.

Inter-alia, however, when the curtain came down on the final performance of *How's The World Treating You?* it unfortunately also marked the end of a very short-lived rebirth of the original Theatre 77 company. It was a tense time. There was always a type of dissatisfied rumble going on back stage throughout rehearsals and during the run of the play. It has been suggested that there were too many over-inflated egos to allow for peaceful creative coexistence, certainly for any kind of cohesion. There is probably something plausible, accurate even, in that notion. The fact remains – neither Sydney nor Billy ever acted at The Barn again. Neither did Pat Priestley nor Pam Hitchens, and Grace now totally disappeared from the scene. Newer recruit Vin McKie went on to appear in Sam Hillary's *Koo Koo* in 1968 and Trevor Rhone's *School's Out* in 1974. Andrew Garbutt, outrageously funny in *What the Butler Saw*, appeared also in the *Shakespeare for Schools* production directed by Sam Walters,[6] both productions having been presented in 1971.

The big question which faced the group was where were the plays to feed this hungry little lion of a theatre? We could find few scripts that appealed to us. At the time, we were aware of few plays that either interpreted or explored the contemporary political and social concerns of Jamaicans. The company had looked abroad in the first instance and produced *How's The World Treating You?*, but we had decided we could not continue along this path. A direct result of this decision was the inauguration of a series of sessions in which interested actors could join in workshops where they were encouraged to devise ad hoc scenes in the vain hope we might stumble upon the beginnings of a new relevant Jamaican play.

In tribute to Rose Bruford, these were call "devising workshops".

Devising was not an original idea. At Rose Bruford College, one of the more popular challenges was the devising of plays from ideas which the students found relevant to their lives and the society they were part of. The results of a devised session were recorded, transcribed. To this end, we somehow found, were given – I doubt we bought it – a large unwieldy Grundig reel-to-reel tape recorder, which weighed a ton. This grey monster was put to constant use recording the workshop sessions.

Eventually people outside the charmed circle of Theatre 77 members, for instance Daryll Crosskill, a one time student of Trevor's at Kingston College, and Sonia Mills (then Manderson) were invited to join these sessions in which the imagination was given full flight. Many other talented members of the theatrical community including Melba Bennett, Janet Bartley,[7] Joanna Hart were contributors to these blue-skies play-making sessions.

Trevor was the person who struggled home with the Grundig where he spent hours transcribing the work which had been recorded. Big job. Hard work. He soon began editing the more useful scenes, those with the most potential, for further workshopping by the company.

I think it was during this process that the playwright Trevor Rhone was born.[8] I am not aware of anything of substance written by him before 1966. It is probably safe to suggest that without the Theatre 77 Barn experience, Trevor Rhone might not have become the playwright he did, Munair Zacca would not be the "grand old man" of Jamaican theatre he now is[9] and there is no doubt in my mind that a fifty-year career of directing theatre internationally would not have been on the cards for me.

In the mean time, we had to find plays to put on, to keep the energy going. We could not countenance the idea of Theatre 77 as a flash in the pan. Many members of the literary community were on our side and some of the more generous gave practical as well as philosophical support. One consequence was the first half of the next offering at The Barn, a double bill, *On the Off Beat*, featuring poetic works by four Jamaican writers. The second half of this programme was a staged dramatization of Langston Hughes' *Ask Your Mama*. The writers read their work in dramatized performance.

Writers, least of all poets, were not then accustomed to reading their work in public, quite common place as it is these days. They were very self-conscious to begin with. Even Dennis Scott,[10] who was quite happy dancing in public, had his moments of doubt, but as rehearsals went on one could almost feel the relaxation setting in and very soon we experienced the confidence of these four talented men of letters, expertly lit, as they read either from a lectern or struck poses on a large piece of dramatic looking drift wood from the easterly parish of St. Thomas, meant to symbolize the spirit of rebel heroes such as Three Finger Jack, Paul Bogle and George William Gordon.

The brave writers who subjected themselves to this ordeal were, John Hearne (1926-1994),[11] well known Jamaican educator, novelist, journalist and friend of Roger Mais, Dennis Scott, Basil McFarlane[12] who belonged to a family of distinguished Jamaican poets, his father J .E. Clare McFarlane having been Jamaica's first poet Laureate, and our recent Poet Laureate, Mervyn Morris[13] (now Lorna Goodison), Rhodes Scholar, Emeritus Professor of Creative Writing and West Indian Literature at the University of the West Indies where he has taught since the 1960s, sadly the only member of that group still alive. Mervyn Morris has been a staunch supporter and important recorder of Jamaican theatre for as long as one can remember. When asked to share a memory or two of the 1966 performance of the poets, he had it seemed, great pleasure in admitting the only thing he could remember was the glorious sight of Cheryl Ryman's legs in *Ask your Mama,* much to the delight of his wife, Helen.

Another great Jamaican, painter Karl Parboosingh[14] also fell under the spell of Cheryl's famous legs, as will be enlarged upon later.

Of the four *On the Off Beat* poets, one became an important contributor to the early success of The Barn project, the late lamented Dennis Scott (1939-1991). The following year, 1967, saw the production of one of his very first plays, the one act, *The Inquisitors* directed by Trevor Rhone and featuring Munair Zacca in the cast. Dennis then went on the direct Trevor's *Smile Orange* in 1971 to great critical acclaim. Three years later in 1974 he directed Slade Hopkinson's[15] *Sala* which the playwright referred to as "a kind of comedy". Scott's final appearance at The Barn was in 1976 when he directed Carmen Tipling's *The Skeleton Inside,* after which we lost him to the United States of America.

Scott was poet, (winner of the Commonwealth Poetry Prize in 1976), playwright, actor, dancer, editor, educator both at home in Jamaica, where he held the post of Director of the Jamaica School of Drama, and at Yale University where he was head of Directing from 1986 until his death in 1991. It is important to note that as one of the now acknowledged major influences on the direction of Jamaican and Caribbean plays, Dennis Scott, cut his directorial teeth in 1971 on a Trevor Rhone play, *Sleeper,* at The

Barn. I have always regretted that only one of Dennis Scott's marvellous plays, *The Inheritors*, was ever produced at The Barn. One must take solace from the fact that it was one of his first, if not his very first play and, as such, fulfilled a Barn Theatre objective of empowering first-time writers.

The poetry recital/performance element of *On the Off Beat*, with a playing time of between forty and forty-five minutes, required us to find something else to produce for a good evening's entertainment. George Carter,[16] founder member of Jamaica's Little Theatre Movement (Mr. Carter, as I still think of him), was Jamaica's leading lighting designer and had worked in theatre in Jamaica for as long as any of us could remember. He was always willing to help with theoretical notions, giving practical and searingly accurate criticism.

He had, until that moment, never been asked to direct anything on the stage except the lighting, but we held his total knowledge of theatre in high esteem and it seemed quite natural to ask him to direct the poets, together with the "script" which he had brought to our attention: a tone poem, "Cultural Exchange", by the African American poet Langston Hughes. It was a highly political jazz poem of not more than sixty lines, some of which had only one word. The poem had not, perhaps, been intended for performance, but that did not deter George Carter. His stage and lighting effects were only outgunned by his keen perception and understanding of the piece. Officially called "Cultural Exchange", he used its secondary title "Ask Your Mama" at The Barn. There were lines in this piece that spoke volumes to those of us who had had the experience of being black in a white world especially:

> You know, right at Christmas
> They asked me if my blackness,
> Would it rub off?
> I said, Ask Your Mama

On The Off Beat was now secure and neatly packaged. Four Jamaican poets neatly linked with one of America's finest. "Ask Your Mama", lit, designed and directed by George Carter made use of four chairs as the complete set (quite daring in those days) employing movement, mime and music as disciplines in an evocative sound-scape designed by Del Weller, to create a perfect evening's visually delightful physical theatre. The lighting effects included state of the art equipment not ordinarily available in Jamaica... a moving electronic wheel, projecting spinning coloured lights, complicated gobos.[17] Mr. Carter went all out on this one. At his own expense.

The actors were, predictably, Munair Zacca, Trevor Rhone, Yvonne Jones but we were joined by a beautiful young Cheryl Ryman,[18] who danced us to glory.

Cheryl remembers:

…the photographs of the foundation actors/directors on the side walls of the theatre in those early days and my dream to have my photograph up there one day. I remember thinking that I was part of something really large, innovative and ambitious in Jamaican theatre. The productions were unusual, the packaging of multiple/mixed Arts: well-known poets, dancing and a skit or two thrown in for good measure. Then added to all this was the concept of being economically viable as an artist in theatre by 1977… and to top it all off, I was given an opportunity to be working with people whom I respected and was a little in awe of.

Rehearsals at The Barn were lively occasions often throwing up more opinions than there were people. Some of the more enlightened folk in the community used to sneak in at the back and watch what was going on. Two of these were Karl Parboosingh and Douglas Manley[19] who would offer valid, sometimes playful, suggestions, once in a while. Karl loved what he saw especially "Ask Your Mama".

Cheryl again:

I remember being in the remount of "Ask Your Mama" – Karl Parboosingh loved that production and The Barn so much that he offered to mount a mural created by him on the facia of the back part of the "garage" (I think that was in front/above the stage). His one proviso for "payment" was that we remount that play to mark the unveiling of his work. That was very exciting.

On 23rd September 1967, a large mural some twenty-four feet at its widest point spanning the entire width of The Barn was unveiled as a gift to the theatre from Karl Parboosingh. This powerful work painted mainly in black and white with telling splashes of red had been inspired by the performance of "Ask Your Mama". It was a homage to Langston Hughes who had died during May of that year: The mural was the work of Jamaican artist of Sikh origin.

Culture, they say, is a two-way street: Langston Hughes.

Our audiences were appreciative and growing in number. The hunt was always on for something to give them, something to titillate. Trevor had this poem which he had jotted down as a result of seeing two unemployed young men leaning on a lamppost in Cross Roads, I seem to remember. Looking for work? It was called *Look Two*. It was very short, not even five minutes in length, and we considered as a possible curtain raiser, but to what?

Roger Mais'[20] sister, Jessie Days, at the instigation of John Hearne, told us she might have some of his manuscripts in a box hidden away somewhere and would we like to have a browse through. We found a short play, a heightened, non-realistic drama, rather short on drama but long on importance, recalled by John Hearne as a lost treasure from Mais, whom he regarded as a Jamaican icon. Titled "Rolando and Rosamund", we though it could maybe form part of an event, but we were still short of a complete evening's entertainment. Dennis Scott came up with his first short play, "The Inquisitors", and a triple bill was born. This luxuriated under the title of *Xperiment*. It opened in July 1967.

The Barn was then host to many actors who now play important roles in the development of modern Jamaican culture such as Lennie Little-White[21] and Cheryl Ryman who played the leads. I directed but am forced to admit I remember not a word of this play. In this triple bill, Munair played both men in *Look Two* to some acclaim. As the director of this piece I was worried that a Jamaican of Syrian extraction might have difficulty in being convincing as two poor, out-of-work young black Jamaican men. But I need not have worried. He still can do this piece at the drop of a hat nearly half century later and one still believes him.

Endnotes

1. Kay Osbourne's play deals with the crisis in a working-class black family in a sufferer community. The play was revived in 2006 by Marcia Brown Productions as still socially relevant. Kay Osbourne is the author of other plays such as "Country Duppy", "Children, Children", "Feminine Justice", "Single Entry" and "Rosetta". She has served as general manager for Television Jamaica (TVJ). See ryanbpatrick.blogspot.co.uk/2006/06/wipe-that-smile-remains-socially.htm.

2. Coal pot: a small portable metal circular pot with a grill, fired by charcoal, the traditional Jamaican version of a barbeque if you like. Used chiefly in those days for the roasting of breadfruits.

3. Alwin Bully, from Dominica, worked for many years in Jamaica as Program Specialist for Culture at UNESCO. His plays include *Good*

Morning Miss Millie, *Streak*, *The Ruler*, *Folk Nativity*, *The Nite Box*, *Green Gold*, *Pelé* and a radio serial *Fire Go Bun*. He taught at the Edna Manley School for Visual and Performing Arts. For a more detailed bio and interview, see Olivier Stephenson, *Visions and Voices: Conversations with Fourteen Caribbean Playwrights* (Leeds: Peepal Tree, 2013), pp. 79-110.

4. Originally an actor, Eugene Williams came from humble beginnings in an East Coast Demerara village in Guyana. He was a key member of the Theatre Guild in Georgetown, both acting and directing. He studied at the Jamaican School of Drama in 1976. He received the Best Director award from Actor Boy Awards and a Silver Musgrave medal. See "Award Winning Director Eugene Williams recalls humble beginnings", *Stabroek News* 8 Sept. 2012 (online).

5. Now Dr. Pamela Mordecai, recipient of a Bronze Musgrave Medal in October 2013, awarded for merit in the field of literature. She is the author of *Journey Poem*, *de Man: A Performance Poem*, *Certifiable*, *The True Blue of Islands*, *Subversive Sonnets*; short stories, *Pink Icing* and a novel, *Red Jacket*. (In 1941 Sir Anthony Musgrave founder of the Institute of Jamaica and one time Governor of the island founded the annual awarding of medals (Gold, Silver and Bronze) to Jamaican citizens who had excelled in the arts and sciences.)

6. Sam Walters (1939-), the founder and Artistic Director of the Orange Tree Theatre in Richmond says this theatre was born in a pub in 1967, soon after his return from Jamaica. He remained Artistic Director until 2014, when he was hailed as the longest serving director in Britain, whose work spanned the world cannon, directing well over one hundred plays. He was awarded an MBE in 1999.

7. Janet Bartley worked on many improvisations at The Barn before memorably playing Elsa in *The Harder They Come*. It was her first film and led to roles in two Michael Abbensett television programmes, *Empire Road* and *Black Christmas*. She married cinematographer David McDonald and had two boys. She died suddenly in London of an aneurism in the 1980s.

8. For a more extensive biography and lengthy interview with Trevor Rhone, see *Visions and Voices*, pp. 237-256.

9. Munair Zacca (1945-), actor, director and playwright. Zacca's performance as Corporal Lestrade in Walcott's *Dream on Monkey Mountain* (1975) for the National Festival Theatre of Jamaica is his highlight. He appeared in films such as *Live and Let Die*, *Countryman* and *Shottas*. He had a leading part in the long-running Jamaican

TV serial, *Royal Palm Estate*. For a detailed bio see *The Jamaican Theatre: Highlights...*, pp. 331-334.

10. Dennis Scott (1939-1991) was a distinguished poet, dramatist, actor and lecturer. From 1977-1983 he was Director of the Jamaican School of Drama; a Visiting Professor in Directing at the Yale School of Drama, and Acting Chairman. His plays include *The Crime of Anabel Campbell*, *An Echo in the Bone*, *Dog* and *Live and Direct from Babylon*. His books of poetry are *Uncle Time*, *Dreadwalk*, *Strategies* and *After-Image* (edited Mervyn Morris. Leeds: Peepal Tree, 2008).

11. John Hearne (1926-1994) was a fine Jamaican novelist and journalist. His novels include: *Voices Under the Window*, *Stranger at the Gate*, *The Faces of Love*, *The Autumn Equinox*, *The Land of the Living* and *The Sure Salvation*.

12. Basil McFarlane (1922-2000) was a poet and journalist who worked for *The Gleaner* and Radio Jamaica. He published a collection: *Jacob and the Angel and Other Poems*, and was quite widely anthologised.

13. Mervyn Morris (1937-) is the author of the poetry collections *The Pond, On Holy Week, Shadow Boxing, Examination Centre, I Been There, Sort of: New and Selected Poems* and *Collected Poems*; and the critical works: *Is English We Speaking, Making West Indian Literature* and *Miss Lou: Louse Bennett and Jamaican Culture*.

14. Karl Parboosingh, celebrated Jamaican artist (1923-1975) studied at the Arts Students League in New York, at the Ecole des Beaux-Arts, Paris, and at the Instituto Nacional de Bellas Artes in Mexico. He returned to Jamaica in 1953.

15. Abdhur-Rahman Slade Hopkinson (1934-1993), Guyanese playwright poet, actor and academic studied at the University College of the West Indies alongside Derek Walcott and Mervyn Morris, colleague of Jan Carew. His *Spawning of Eel* was written as *Sala* in 1968. His selected poetry was published as *Snowscape with Signature* (Leeds: Peepal Tree Press, 1993).

16. George Carter (1916-2016) *The Cambridge Guide to African and Caribbean Theatre* records that for 40 years he worked on every important theatre productions in Jamaica – including the annual pantomime. He was awarded a Silver Musgrave in 1972 and an Order of Distinction in 1977. See *The Cambridge Guide...*, p. 206.

17. Gobos are templates or stencils used to shape stage lighting.

18. Cheryl Ryman was the principal dancer at the National Dance Theatre Company of Jamaica (c1967), scholar, academic, lecturer and author of many important papers on the Jamaican Heritage in Dance.

19. Son of Jamaica's Prime Minister Norman Manley and brother of Michael.
20. Roger Mais (1905-1955) Jamaican novelist, poet, painter, journalist, playwright and, for a time, political activist. In 1944, he served six months in prison on a charge of sedition. His novels include *The Hills Were Joyful*, *Brother Man* and *Black Lightning*. His published plays included *The First Sacrifice* and *George William Gordon*, and many unpublished and unperformed short plays. Posthumously awarded the Order of Jamaica in 1978.
21. Lennie Little-White; producer/director creator of Mediamix Jamaica's premier media house who, as a young man, "flirted" with the idea of doing professional theatre until this was abandoned in favour of film in the late 60s.

CHAPTER FOUR: THE EXPANDING ROLE OF THE BARN

Personal roles within Theatre 77 were beginning to find a synthesis. Although we three filled in gaps where necessary, the growing reality was that Trevor was writing, Munair was acting and Yvonne was directing. As time went on, marketing and publicity strategies, which had at first been all but ignored, now had to be properly designed and executed if we were to succeed, to consolidate our small successes.

Marketing was not the science it now is. Our marketing strategy, if one could call it that, was to cobble together some large bits of wood, paint them black and in white writing announce the next play at The Barn. These monsters were lashed with wire to the telephone and electricity poles which flourished in abundance in Kingston. It must be said that these large wooden billboards often disappeared overnight. Some were later seen as doors to makeshift housing. Sometimes we also used bits of tin, but these were less effective and also had a way of disappearing.

We managed to wheedle a number of interviews with the *Gleaner* and the *Star* newspapers, resulting in a fair amount of editorial. Headlines such as "Wants Professional theatre for Jamaica" occasionally stared out from the social and entertainment pages, but the content was usually rather tongue-in-cheek. The maxim "No publicity is bad publicity" was a kind of salve to our bruised egos.

We were also quietly hoping to attract at least a few of Paul Methuen's Garden Theatre people to our offerings, by hanging around on the fringes, trying to chat up members of the audience in the intervals. This ploy was successful to some extent, as we enticed people like Gillian and Graham Binns to spread the work in the expatriate community. Leonie Forbes was also very helpful as were Paul Methuen himself, Louise Bennett and Lois Kelly Barrow.

The Clarkes of 5 Oxford Road had by now grown accustomed to cars being parked on the lawn, in their driveway. Strangers peering in at the windows of their home were somehow almost part of the exciting experiment, although they would have hotly denied this.

One day a truck drew up and off-loaded sixty new chairs. Trevor always said: "Mrs Clarke[1] was our mentor and our threshold guardian." She had grown weary of sitting on the floor, even when cushioned. She also had a soft spot for Trevor. I think this feeling was mutual. The evening before he died, on the 15th September 2009, Trevor spent two whole hours holding her 97-year-old hands, heads together, talking to her in whispers.

So now, anyway, there were chairs.

There were other activities developing too. Round about this time, early in 1968, regular Saturday morning drama classes for children took place in and around the theatre in an attempt to train our audiences of the future.[2] A small industry of training young people in all the arts of theatre, both physical and practical, developed almost by default. The late George Silvera was a classic graduate ambassador who, at the time of his death, was a highly regarded technical director in Jamaican theatre. Shows for children were produced, the best remembered being *Ali Baba*. There were also classes in many aspects of theatre, even some in stage make-up, led by Sheila Burke. These Saturday morning classes came to an end in 1974.

Yvonne and children at The Barn

The Barn became, almost by default, a meeting place for creative artists from all disciplines. In 1968, a small kiln for firing ceramics was imported and installed, creating a makeshift studio called Back-o'-the-Barn Ceramics. Edna Manley,[3] in her generosity, taught the novices the necessary technique of firing pots in the kiln. A 23 year old Gene Pearson[4] was invited to take up residence in the first years of his life as a ceramicist, as was Jean Taylor.[5] Both of these talented artists worked behind The Barn for years and held successful exhibitions of their work in the theatre, notable among them Gene Pearson's in 1969 and Jean Taylor's in May 1971. It is instructive to note, in the many citations which abound, that the formative experience that the humble Barn provided to the young Pearson, at no cost to him, is never mentioned. I, however, treasure the first pot he ever threw and fired in the famous kiln: imperfect in orange and green glaze, sporting many unintentional bulges and cracks, but so full of life.

Unfortunately, Back-o'-the-Barn Ceramics closed its doors in June 1971. The space was ultimately too small, too ramshackle; the kiln was getting old and dangerous. 1971 was, anyway, the year when the first innovative and inventive period of the theatre's life begun to take on a different perspective. It was now five years old.

Karl Parboosingh has already been mentioned as a regular visitor at rehearsals, and generous donor of his fine mural. Young artists Christopher Gonzales[6] and Dawn Scott[7] used to live in Norwood Avenue, which ran alongside The Barn, and often stopped to say hello on their way up and down the road, often hanging out and helping with the scene painting. John Banks, then a young, handsome devil pilot of The Jamaica Defence Force, took to buzzing the place from his cockpit when bored…

There was also an interesting development in the socio-economic make-up of the audiences, which began with *Look Two*. Our initial audiences were mostly uptown theatre types, many of whom were slumming it for the excitement of something new – which they might, at best, be able to parody. Many were chauffeur driven. When we began to see the heads of the chauffeurs outside the theatre jostling for space at the back windows, peeping in to get a taste of what was going on, it stirred something fundamental.

"Look Two" was the first performance to catch their imagination, and on the Sunday afternoon performances we began to notice a marked change in the composition of the audience. Those who had been peeping in at the windows from outside during weeknight performances, were now buying tickets and arriving with their ladies dressed to kill on Sunday afternoons. No sitting on cushions on the floor for these ladies. Thank goodness for the chairs.

This audience development was inspiring, and anxious to maintain the new patrons' interest, there was a fair amount of pressure on Trevor to produce something from all those improvisations, something that could be put on stage, something which would have more relevance, to be crude, to the chauffeurs. We knew the imagination of the man in the street needed to be fed as much as that of the usual theatre suspects. We had to begin exploring ways of engaging with the culture and experience of the Jamaican "man in the street".

Even so, we had to continue seeking out existing material to produce for our growing audience while we waited for the play, "our" play to emerge.

In London, during the summer of 1967, I attended a lunchtime performance of Ed Bullins' new one act play, *The Electronic Nigger* at the Ambiance lunch time theatre venue in Bayswater run by Trinidadian Junior Telfer. There were not many in the audience, but I found myself captivated by the modernity and political acuity of this short play. At the end of the performance I turned to the man sitting close by and said: "This is a marvellous play. I am sure it would go down well in Jamaica. I wonder how I could get the rights?"

The man answered in a slow drawl: "Well honey, it's all yours!"

My neighbour turned out to be Ed Bullins, writer in residence at the Lafayette Theatre in New York.[8] The seven character play was presented with four actors in London as was the production at The Barn.

The title *The Electronic Nigger* caused hiccups in some circles as should have been anticipated, perhaps. Briefly, the plot goes: Ray Jones, described as a light brown-skinned man, is a part-time evening class lecturer in a Creative Writing class. He does this job for the money as his first novel has been a disaster. He needs to eat. He is a regular guy. In his class is A.T. Carpentier who is described as "very dark" and who never stops talking, which he does in an affected manner, with lines such as: "the new technology doesn't allow for the work tyranny of human attitudes…"

Carpentier, who insists on the French pronunciation of his name and whose opinions appear extremely right wing, has a motive. By affecting to be what one character calls "a completely white-washed man" he manages to destroy middle-of-the road, predictable, Ray Jones' credibility. The outcome is that Carpentier takes over the class. It was one of those plays which make you laugh while feeling guilty about doing so, and in this manner drives home the burden of the play: the need for reform of the education system. Although the play relates to the North American situation it resonated well in Jamaica.

This play provoked drama off stage and as well as on. Robert Hill, now a distinguished academic and pivotal source of knowledge on C.L.R. James, was a hot-headed youngster at the time, like a lot of us, and he picketed the theatre in objection to the title of the play which, had he read the play, he may not have done.

More recently (2013) in the UK city of Liverpool, Professor Hill was the keynote speaker in a conference on the life and work of C.L.R. James. I also happened to be giving a short paper at the conference and took the opportunity to remind him of his youthful picketing occasion. We had a good laugh at our younger selves.

While in London, yet another play was identified which might fit the bill for production at The Barn. This was another one act play, *Neighbours*, written by an English playwright James Saunders, a prolific writer whose plays were marked by a tendency to be rather abstract. *Neighbours* had received its first professional production at the Hampstead Theatre in May 1967 and transferred to the West End as part of a double bill with Leroi Jones' (now Amiri Baraka) *Dutchman*. The characters in *Neighbours* are called simply Man and Woman. Man is aggressive, arrogant with an enormous chip on his shoulder. Woman is nervous, tentative. The play is really a conversation between a black man and a white woman as they try to address the gulf between them which colour presents. It is a naturalistic play set in a small sitting room. In the London production Calvin Lockhart played Man with distinction. In Kingston, due to circumstances beyond our control, Munair Zacca played Man as he records below. It was not a success. Munair remembers:

> There was *Neighbours* by James Saunders, directed by Yvonne and Trevor. I recall that when the actor cast as the man in this two-hander was required to kneel to the girl, he absolutely refused to do so and left the production. This was two weeks from opening, and who was called on to replace him? None other than the resident actor at The Barn: moi... MZ! Well, to tell the truth, this was one of the worst acting jobs I ever had.

Meanwhile, back at The Barn, we were told that young Daryll Crosskill, Sonia Manderson (Mills) and Trevor were working-up one of the devised pieces into a full length play. Towards the latter part of 1967, the first draft of the play was ready. It was called *It's Not My Fault, Baby*. This was the first full-length Jamaican play that was mounted at The Barn, credited finally to a trio of writers: Daryll Croskill, Trevor Rhone and Jackson Martin. I knew Jackson Martin had been Sonia Manderson Mills' *nom de plume* and it was she who had written a lot of the play. When asked recently for any comment she might like to make on the exercise, she did not have much to say except that she had been quite unaware that anyone else had been working on the script except her. It seems Trevor had not shared this fact with her. The play dealt forcibly with the socio-political and financial difficulties of those returning from study abroad, who in many cases were ridiculed, and exploited.

Munair Zacca remembers again:

A production which is etched in the brain is *It's Not My Fault, Baby* – I
so loved and relished playing the character of Ron in this play and could've
gone on and on,

The cast of eight included Trevor as well as Munair and Cheryl and
myself. Some new actors appeared, among them Melba Bennett, Roy
Case, Tess Thomas and Stan Irons, who were to become familiar faces
on The Barn stage. Fraught nerves were also very much a part of this
production. The directorial credits were given to three people: George
Carter, Trevor and me, but the remembered truth is that it was a bit
of a free-for-all. Experts proliferated. Disagreements reigned, but not
supremely.

The setting was pretty rudimentary, with a large platform in the middle
of the stage, much too generous for this tiny space, with the other settings
ending up being bare and symbolic. However, this play was the whetstone
for the future policy of the Theatre 77, or The Barn Theatre, which was
how people were now calling it. "Must be Local" and "Must be Immediate"
were the catch phrases which neatly encapsulated the artistic policy.

This was also one of those tense times. There were many tense times.
Tempers began to unravel, once to the extent of Trevor ordering me to
leave the theatre one early evening… and not return. Major turbulence as
he would say. This happened after a particularly intense disagreement on
some quite minor issue. Not unusual. I was living at home so I didn't have
far to go. When I appeared so early from rehearsals, my parents were mildly
interested. I told them I had been exiled from The Barn by Trevor. My
mother was quite aerated: "But how can he exile you? This is not like
Trevor…", and so on and on and on. My father, however, was quite silent.
He was not as enamoured with Trevor as my mother was. His reaction to
the exile was quite different. As a land surveyor, it didn't take long for him
to arrange to have the land on which The Barn stood officially converted
into a new and separate title in my name. I had no idea he had done this.
Eventually, just before he died, he said, quite casually: "You can now tell
him to leave your property if you wish."

Theatre breeds drama.

The simple truth is I didn't really mind the exile which didn't last that
long anyway. Spending all my waking hours in The Barn, when I wasn't
teaching at Melbourne, was getting more than a little claustrophobic. I now
had an excuse to be absent, to think about, to dream about charting my own

life in theatre, not in Jamaica, but far away in England. I dreamt of doing Jamaican work in London which was bursting with Jamaican migrants. The exile was short lived: Trevor needed the keys to the place. All was forgiven and my thoughts of setting London alight returned to the back boiler – for a while.

Writing full length plays on demand is a difficult task. But somehow Trevor had been bitten by the writing bug and begun working on a one act play, *Yes Mama,* which he completed in no time at all. Not his greatest play, it dealt with exploitation of another kind: by a mother of her young nubile daughter. It was acted by Cheryl Ryman, Melba Bennett, Betty Canton and Munair Zacca and directed by Yvonne Jones. To this was added a topical revue *I'm Human, Right?* This solicited skits from all and sundry. Graham Binns, the British expatriate General Manager at Radio Jamaica, my boss, and a one time member of the Oxford University Drama Society (OUDS) in England, contributed quite a few.

We asked distinguished Jamaican choreographer Neville Black, one time member of the National Dance Theatre Company of Jamaica, home from choreographing in Chicago, to direct it. With eight members, the cast included two new faces as well as the usual suspects: Raymond Hill, an ex student at Kingston College, probably the best mime Jamaica has ever produced, who died much too young, and Gladstone Wilson, now of radio and legal fame. Trevor's one act play, together with the revue, formed yet another double bill. Neville proved an excellent director and, of course, the movement was superb, as were the costumes, which I believe he designed.

Finding suitable plays to produce remained a challenge and we scoured all the sources we knew. This was before the world wide web made such research relatively easy. Emails were things of the future; one had to rely on expensive phone calls or letters which took ages to reach destinations, or better yet, on bush telegraph.

Sam Hillary[90] a quietly spoken, non-excitable, nice Jamaican gentleman was someone whom we all respected and wanted to work with. He had had a great success with the script for *Banana Boy* in 1961, reputably one of the most successful of the Jamaican pantomime genre. His play *Chippy* is regarded as a Jamaican classic. We had in interviews with the press, blithely said we wanted to work with him, but it was Rex Nettleford, Founder and Artistic Director of the National Dance Theatre Company of Jamaica, who introduced the Hillary play *Koo Koo* to us. This sort of generous interplay between established figureheads in the arts and The Barn was beginning to happen more often. The support was needed and appreciated.

Munair remembers *Koo Koo:*

This was a script by Sam Hillary… directed by you, Yvonne, with Trevor, myself, Vin McKie and that English girl Libby [Elizabeth Joyce] as the cast. I seem to recall I was quite aroused at first when I shared my first stage-kiss, ha! I also remember that you made me cry on account of your very critical comments regarding how I was playing the role. I intensely disliked the character type, and I guess at this early stage of my career I hadn't yet learned how to separate personal feelings from the work itself.

Koo Koo played successfully at The Barn in 1968, but always looming in the background was the constant worry: What to do next as we waited for Trevor to come up with a new play? Answers came there few. In desperation we went back to the English cannon and embarked on producing Harold Pinter's one-act comedy of supposed infidelity, *The Collection* (1961), which was another mistake. The cast (Trevor Rhone, Munair Zacca, Mike Lewis and an exuberant Joanna Hart) were very good but the play did not speak to the audience.

Having been at drama school in England sometimes led us into cultural confusion in our mission to change the world of Jamaican theatre; in England, Pinter was the bread and butter option when in doubt, and with this in mind we programmed his *Collection* as a stopgap. This was a flop. A misjudgment in the changing tastes of our audience which had been quite quickly getting accustomed to Jamaican-flavoured productions and this one did not even begin to cut the mustard. The cast consists of two middle class English couples, James and Stella, and Harry and Bill. The central theme is the possibility of Stella and Bill having had night of extramarital sex while away on business. This is plausible and possible as they are both dress designers. One never quite knows whether this is an elaborate hoax cooked up by one of characters or whether the seduction did or did not take place. A typical Pinter deadly serious sexual comedic romp which might go down quite well in Jamaica now, in the first quarter of the 21st century. With all the illicit bed-hopping and so on I can see it adapted and abridged for the present day Jamaican audience and having a roaring success. However, it fell flat then back in the late 1960s. Live and learn from our mistakes is how we consoled ourselves. One positive outcome though was that lovely talented Joanna Hart, who went on to have a long career in Jamaican theatre, was introduced to the company.

Endnotes

1. The Barn in Kathleen Clarke's words: "Before long my daughter had taken up with Trevor Rhone. They were inseparable – "batty and bench" as we say – much to the disgust of Claude who thought poor Trevor was pompous, sly, and "over-ripe" – whatever that meant. I didn't mind the lad as he worked hard. The difference in his background was a plus in my eyes, however beyond the pale it was in most others. I always tried to support their efforts to activate and politicise the local theatre scene which was dominated at the time by some "big no dough" white people who thought that their tastes were by some heavenly ordinance, superlative.

2. The Barn Theatre for Children produced *Dorothy Donkey* by Barbara Gloudon as well as a mime *Anancy Story* in 1973 under the guidance of Belinda Durity. See Kole Omotoso, *The Theatrical into Theatre*.

3. Edna Manley sculptor, painter, ceramicist of distinction, wife of the Jamaican Prime Minister Norman Manley. Her journal, *Focus*, published a number of plays.

4. Gene Pearson, CD, Silver Musgrave medallist 2010. Internationally fashionable sculptor especially of his signature of Nubian heads.

5. Later Jean Taylor-Bushay, she ran Studio Potters. See "Ceramics in Jamaica: An Overview", *Arts Jamaica*, vol 3 nos 1 & 2, Nov. 1984, p. 10.

6. Christopher Gonzales OD 1943-2008, celebrated Jamaican sculptor and painter. His celebrated and imaginative sculpture of Bob Marley was loathed by many Jamaicans and withdrawn.

7. Dawn Scott 1951-2010 artist, designer, activist. Awarded a Bronze Musgrave medal in 1999.

8. Ed Bullins was for a time Minister of Culture for the Black Panthers. Other Ed Bullins plays include, amongst the 47 he wrote: *Goin' a Buffalo, In the Wine Time, A Son, Come Home, Clara's Ole Man*. He was awarded an Obe for *The Taking of Miss Janice*.

9. Sam Hillary (1936-). His other plays include *Departure in the Dark* (1960) and *Chippy* (1965), both once regularly performed across the region.

CHAPTER FIVE: THE NINETEEN-SEVENTIES

The seventies was a most productive innovative decade for the theatre.

Ken Maxwell belonged to one of the very old families, which had originally arrived in Jamaica from Scotland. Over the centuries they integrated and identified completely with the Jamaican ethic; some might say influenced it. He was in fact really a gentleman farmer from Mandeville in the heart of the Jamaican countryside, but his influence came from his extremely popular radio programmes as a social commentator and comedian who used his alter ego, Pro Rata Powell, to say the politically unthinkable. In 1970, having written a number of successful revues, under the umbrella name of *Please… Soon Come Please, Yes Please* and so on, offered to do one for us.

Trevor, Munair and I were really intending, hoping, aspiring to produce meaningful realistic dramas based on the Jamaican condition but, as we discovered, these things take time. We welcomed Ken's *Soon Come Please* with open arms. Although much of it was, in retrospect, rather undergraduate humour there were one or two telling moments of political comment. Unfortunately, this revue failed to find favour with the critics. The inimitable Barbara Gloudon's critical headline was simply "No Please." Archie Lindo was kinder. He praised the cast but found the scripts somewhat crude. The cast was large for us, nine on some nights, eight on others. Ken Maxwell would turn up if the roads from Mandeville permitted. Tom Cook directed. Ken Cole, Phillip Zinn and a young slim Volier Johnson[1] joined ranks with us for this revue.

In those far off days of the early 70s, life was more personal and immediate. Trevor's brother Neville brought tidings of unrest from the Michael Manley camp in Garth Road, somewhere near the foot of expensive Cherry Gardens Hill residences where his "yet to come" government plotted and planned success. Michael Manley became Prime Minister of Jamaica from 1972 to 1980 and did so again from 1989 to 1992. He was the younger son of Norman Washington Manley QC, Rhodes Scholar, First Chief Minister of Jamaica and National Hero. Wickedly handsome, Michael, a graduate of the London School of Economics, was at the time leader of the

National Workers Union. He was gifted with a pragmatic savviness about how to win the people of Jamaica with music, which he did brilliantly. One remembers turning out on the first Labour Day after his victory at the polls with paint brush and white lime to help beautify the curbs of Kingston's roads, as did numerous others, many of whom were obvious strangers to these implements, but were inspired by the rhetoric of this charismatic man.

But apparently, those in Garth Road, especially Michael Manley, were mightily concerned about one particular sketch in our revue *Soon Come Please* which featured a recent graduate from The London School of Economics who had entered into the trade union business upon returning home. The punch line was that, after having a slap-up lunch with management of "duck under glass", or some such nonsense, while he was meant to be negotiating better pay and conditions for the workers, the union leader returns to inform his followers that he has achieved Music While You Work to blare out on Rediffusion speakers in the factories. Actually, it was not that scurrilous – not even that clever, really.

Michael Manley, reportedly, objected to this sketch and was threatening to take out an injunction to have the theatre closed if we did not cease to perform this item which, incidentally, he had not seen.

I guess, as the person officially responsible for what happened in the theatre building, I was expected to face the wrath of Mr. Manley. I was escorted to Garth Road by Neville Rhone, where Mr. Manley surrounded by at least two of his close allies, Messrs Eric Bell and Hopeton Caven, made his position and intention very clear. Unfortunately, my sense of humour let me down this time, and my unfortunate throw away comment… *If the cap fits, wear it…* resulted in an irate politician who had to be restrained, causing his close associate, Beverly Anderson, who had been monitoring the proceedings from a not-too-distant doorway, to have to intervene, and pacify, which she did successfully.

We did not cut the sketch from the revue.

There was no injunction.

Jamaica is a small island, and Kingston an even smaller capital city. Even without the aid of modern day cell phones and Facebook, the story spread like wild fire and the show sold out thereafter.

The company did not confine itself solely to operating within the wooden walls of its garage home, but travelled far and wide into the Jamaican countryside. One important strand of this touring arm was the first ever, ground-breaking schools tour in February 1971 of fully rehearsed

excerpts from the three Shakespeare plays which were set texts for the
Senior Cambridge Overseas Examination. Jamaican fifth formers sat
these in those days.

On the syllabus were *Hamlet, Midsummer Night's Dream* and *Julius Caesar*.
This tour was undertaken in response to requests from some secondary
schools. We performed in the majority of secondary schools not only in the
corporate area of Kingston and St. Andrew but in most other twelve
parishes as well. Directed by Sam Walters, a visiting UK theatre director,
who should have been, officially, working for the Little Theatre Movement, the production used a minimal concept to maximum effect. What
Sam was able to get out of his Barn acting team of eight actors was little short
of a miracle. The travelling acting company included Joanna Hart, Janet
Bartley, Andrew Garbutt, Bim Lewis, Peter Ashbourne, Trevor Rhone,
Munair Zacca, and myself.[2]

Peter Ashbourne, Ernest Cromwell and Janet Bartley

I asked Sam Walters, now a highly sought after director in London and
until recently Artistic Director of the Orange Tree Theatre in London, to
write a few words on his memories of this event and of his time in Jamaica
between 1970-1971. He graciously complied, writing this about his and his
wife, Auriol Smith's (co-founder of the Orange Tree) stay:

Although expected to be three years and ending up as only one, our
stay in Jamaica remains an important and memorable time in our lives.
I had been employed by Henry and Greta Fowler to start a Drama

School with the long term aim of creating a professional theatre company under the auspices of the Little Theatre Movement. The reason I got considered for this assignment was that my main acting teacher at drama school in London (LAMDA) was Vivien Matalon, who had first been approached by the Fowlers, but whose career as a director in London was taking off. So he recommended me. The reason that an outsider was approached may have been that Henry and Greta had fallen out with all the contenders already in the country!

I learned a lot very quickly about the relationships within the small Jamaican theatrical community. Not all of it positive. And I remember going to Rex Nettleford for help and advice.

Although my wife Auriol would teach and work in the theatre, she was also employed by Henry to teach some drama at the Priory School, which we lived opposite in a flat of the Fowlers, where we were looked after by the lovely Blossom (Eunice MacLeish) with whom we have, alas, lost contact.

It was a big thing to transport ourselves, our belongings, our about be two years old daughter, Dorcas, and a motor car across the Atlantic but we anticipated a stay of at least 3 years.

I enjoyed setting up the drama school and was hugely fortunate in being guided towards people like Olive Lewin and Eddie Thomas who would come and work with the students, for after all I knew no one.

Two young actors in particular made an immediate impression on me. Janet Bartley we saw almost as soon as we arrived, in a small part in the Pantomime, starring the wonderful Louise Bennett, paired of course with Ranny Williams. I watched them daunted, as I knew the idea was that I might direct the next year's one!

Janet was an instinctive and highly talented actress. She became a friend of mine and my wife's. She starred in the Jimmy Cliff film *The Harder They Come*, where she met her husband and later came to London to study and work. When she died at a cruelly early age I truly believe that we lost someone who could have become a great actress. She was also a lovely person – and a great cook! We miss her a lot.

The other actor was Oliver Samuels. When Oliver auditioned to be in the Drama School he had never set foot on the stage. But as soon as I met with him it was clear that here was a natural talent.

The first production I did was *A Raisin in the Sun* by Lorraine Hansberry, with Buddy Pouyatt, who became a good friend and support, excellent in the main role. And indeed it was a production I was proud of and in which all the cast were extremely good. And this cast included Janet Bartley as Beneatha and Oliver Samuels in a small role.

Oliver went onto play the main part in Brecht's *The Exception and the Rule* which was a part of my ill-fated triple bill.

Having arrived in February 1970, produced *Raisin* and done work with the drama students, including a new play by Dennis Campbell, in the autumn I chose to stage a triple bill of *Go Tell in on Table Mountain* by the Jamaica-born playwright, Evan Jones, now firmly ensconced and

successful in the UK; *Birdbath* by the American playwright, Leonard
Melfi, and the Brecht play.

Attendance at rehearsal for the Brecht had been very bad. In fact
unpunctuality been plaguing me throughout all my work. My exhorting
that the theatre is a co-operative activity and that you can't just not turn
up for a rehearsal, because it destroys everyone else's ability to work, had
fallen on deaf ears. However, I was determined to get my lesson through.

Table Mountain and *Birdbath* – a two-hander with Auriol Smith and
Buddy Pouyatt – were ready to open. The Brecht was not. I changed
the planned order of the plays for nothing could follow the shambles
that I anticipated that the Brecht would be (Oliver Samuels' performance
excepted). The first two plays were excellent and then the Brecht happened.
It was as bad as could be imagined.

At the board meeting which followed the next day, I was reprimanded for
having let the production open. I made my points about discipline and punctuality
and resigned. My time with the Little Theatre Movement was over.

But there were things to tie up, the year to complete, and Yvonne
Brewster (Jones then) came to my rescue and I was delighted to end
my year in Jamaica working for The Barn Theatre.

I had of course met with Yvonne and Trevor Rhone. Both had taught
at the Drama School and I had seen excellent things at The Barn. I had
also started to dream longingly of perhaps trying to create a similar small
theatre back in Richmond, London where we lived, which I did when I
founded the Orange Tree Theatre shortly after my return. So thank you
Barn Theatre for creating the germ of a theatre which still thrives today.

With The Barn we put on shortened versions of *Julius Caesar*, *A Midsummer
Night's Dream* and *Hamlet* which toured to schools as well as, I think,
playing at The Barn. I was particularly pleased with the *Julius Caesar*
which I adapted to involve only the scenes with Brutus (played by Munair
Zacca) showing how he became involved in the conspiracy and its
consequences. The venture was I think a success and led to further such
work being done. I loved the intimacy of The Barn and was very grateful
to be offered this chance to work in such conducive surroundings at a
time when things had gone awry elsewhere.

Later, of course, Yvonne returned to London where she founded the
excellent Talawa Theatre Company and we continued to be friends.

Despite our stay in Jamaica being shorter than expected, and containing
aspects of work that we did not enjoy, there is so much we remember
with love and affection – the Sundays at Buddy Pouyat's (and working
with him too), working with the young Bartley and Samuels, the production
of *A Raisin in the Sun*, watching Olive Lewin and her Jamaican Folksingers
and the National Dance Theatre (who we were able to see again recently
at the Alexandra Theatre in Birmingham), meeting Miss Lou, acquiring
a taste for rum and ginger which I still retain (without, alas, having access
to Desnoes and Geddes ginger ale) and Dorcas naked in her baby swimming
pool with her face covered in mango juice. And of course "Blossom".

Sam.

It might be of interest that Sam's first production at the Orange Tree Theatre in Richmond, London, which he founded soon after his return to the United Kingdom after his baptism of fire in Jamaica, was *Go Tell It on Table Mountain* by Jamaican Evan Jones.

Sam Walters was and still is, in his mid-seventies, an inspired, inspiring, imaginative director celebrated as the mastermind for forty-three years behind the famous Orange Tree Theatre in London and until recently its Artistic Director. He has always been known for his bravery in tackling subjects others had kept well away from, sometimes classical sometimes modern, but always unpredictable, and always good theatre.

The production of Shakespeare extracts was conceived as one which would tour to schools up and down the length of Jamaica, playing in auditoriums as varied in size and amenities as one could imagine. Sam Walters had to come up with a style of production which was highly adaptable and easily transportable. We had only a small van that Peter Ashbourne[3] drove – he says well, but we thought otherwise. He also remembers his "frankly bad playing of a bad conga drum". Joanna Hart can remember nothing of the proceedings, nor can Munair, but Peter is convinced that Trevor's gravitas when delivering "To be or not to be" was something to reckon with. However, what stays with Sam was the reaction of the schoolchildren – ranging from apathy to wild enthusiasm, and the sensitivity and skill of Bim Lewis[4] as Bottom who "always got a good reception".

What Sam did was very cutting edge in those far-off days. A table covered in black was always at the rear of the stage area, on which rested a single prop for each character. A lot of the rehearsal time was spent in exploring this single prop. For Bim, as Bottom the Weaver in the *Dream*, the Shakespearean language came so easily that he couldn't understand why the rest of the cast was making such a song and dance about it all! Actors dressed from head to foot in black made sure their single props were colourful. The experience of loading up the van early in the mornings with Mr. Murray in charge, and George his usual silently watching self, is something that lingers on in the memory.

One or two of the "posher" boarding schools refused to have the touring company visit their schools. I was berated by one headmaster:

> You think I am going to let my boys see this thing you are offering when you have taken the liberty of including a populist stand-up comedian. My God! Bim Lewis, to act in a Shakespearean play? I mean, is he in the cast, really? What would our parents think?

Bim Lewis, the stand-up comic as Bottom, was a bridge too far for this gentleman. Bim Lewis not only understood and spoke the text well, in fact he elucidated it, making it relevant to Jamaicans in his inspired portrayal of Bottom the weaver. How times have changed! An ironic statistic: the pass rate in English literature, especially for the paper on *A Midsummer Night's Dream*, I dare say, shot up markedly in the schools in which we were welcomed.

In that year, March 1971, another professional theatre couple from England, Eileen and Jonathan Porter, came to Jamaica. They had been working at the Manchester Library Theatre. They introduced us to the outrageously anarchic Joe Orton's *What the Butler Saw* ("licensed insanity") only months after it had been premièred in London, as a possible distraction from the usual meaningful (read serious) Barn offerings. The ageing student in us both loved the idea and we somehow managed to get the Porters out to Jamaica, Eileen to direct it and Jonathan to design.

It has been said that the design for this play was one of the most effective ever to grace the tiny stage. It certainly made the best use of the miniature stage (now approximately 24ft wide by 17 feet deep with no wing space to speak of and a raked ceiling which was precariously low) and it cleverly enabled the six members of the cast (Janet Bartley, Andrew Garbutt, Ernest Cromwell, Trevor, Munair, and myself) to move madly about with great ease. There was even a loft on stage. This was a fun play to programme and fun was had by all while we waited for the next Rhone play to emerge. Even the critics were impressed. Mervyn Morris found "madness in symmetry, served with wit." He thought the play "must be one of the cleverest ever written. This production makes us laugh throughout and allows us also to be aware of the meaning that underlie the fun." Harry Milner was kind too. His headline asked whether The Barn production was not better than the one in London!

Endnotes

1. Volier Johnson went on to have a long and successful career in Jamaican theatre and film (including a small part in *The Harder They Come*). He worked with Ed Wallace Productions and Lloyd Reckord, LTM pantomimes and was recognised as a great comic actor. See Mel Cooke, "Volier Johnson Celebrates 40 Years in Theatre", *The Gleaner,* 14 March, 2010.
2. Of this cast Bim Lewis, Trevor Rhone and Janet Bartley have died. Andrew Garbutt is uncontactable, Joanna Hart remembers little,

Munair less. One is therefore grateful for Peter Ashbourne's (now a leading Jamaican classical musician) recollections which are recorded later in the text.)

3. Peter Ashbourne (1950-) is a leading Jamaican musician and composer whose work covers many disciplines including jazz, classical music and reggae. His jazz band Ashes is legendary.

4. Bim Lewis (1914-1976) was half of the famous pair, Bim and Bam (Aston Wynter), the most popular of all the early Jamaican comic duos. Originally a black-face comedy act, they refined in time and developed many shows around Jamaican folk material. These included *Healing in the Balmyard*, *The Black Witch of Trout Hall* and *The Case of John Ras I*. See *The Cambridge Guide to African & Caribbean Theatre*, p. 204.

CHAPTER SIX: TREVOR DAVE RHONE

It was mid 1969 when Trevor completed *The Gadget*, a semi-auto-biographical piece. This was his first full-length play. It came roughly one year since he had written the one acter, *Yes Mama*, but *The Gadget* was what we had been waiting for and was surely worth the wait.

Trevor had struggled with this one. It was sometimes, he said, too close for comfort, too real. In short, the play dealt with the life of a poor boy from the country who, after getting some decent education, has made relatively good in town. His peasant origins and the class prejudices that he has been subjected to, continue to haunt him and ultimately these curtail his adult success. It is a moving play. Especially memorable is Rhone's treatment of how the lead character, Len, tackles the embarrassing memories of the visits his mother makes to him in town, with her head tied in her usual country peasant style, knocking loudly on the gate, bellowing for all the neighbours and especially his stuck up wife to hear: "HOLD DAWG!" When she knows fully well there is no dog.

Rhone's celebrated ability to simultaneously wring tears and laughter from an audience was in its infancy in *Look Two*, becoming more apparent in *Yes Mama*, and taking on a much more assured flight in *The Gadget*.

Trevor shared the direction of the production of *The Gadget* at The Barn with Ancile Gloudon,[1] who was playing a lead part in the play, but always insisted on keeping his name from this directing credit. In my opinion, *The Gadget* is Trevor's seminal play. This is borne out by the fact that he never stopped rewriting it, even after the official, final rewrite of *The Gadget* saw the light of day as *Old Story Time* ten years later, in 1979, when he produced it at the Way Out Theatre, a converted reception room in the Pegasus hotel in New Kingston, just a stone's throw away from The Barn. It would be almost two decades before *Old Story Time* was seen on stage at The Barn in 1997.

Late in 1971, Trevor's greatest success, *Smile Orange*, opened to an excellent reception by audience and critics alike. Brilliantly directed by Dennis Scott, *Smile Orange* broke all box office records and ran at The Barn for a mystical five hundred performances, being sold out most nights. I don't think that record has yet been broken by any other Jamaican play.

Ginger Knight,[2] an ex student at Kingston College who went on to produce several plays at The Barn and who is still writing and producing work for the theatre, wrote:

Did you know that Mr. Trevor Rhone allowed me to watch *Smile Orange* every Sunday for a year (that's right 52 weeks). I stood at the back window. That meant that after a while I knew all the lines and movements, but most importantly I learnt the rhythm... Out of this came "Underwriter's Undercover!"

So what did *Smile Orange* have that appealed to the audiences so emphatically, and still does to this day? There are many schools of thought on this. Michael Manley, in his introduction to one of the anthologies of Rhone's work published by Longman, suggests[3]:

...it was his ear for dialogue, his eye for characterization and his feel for situation which set him apart as a true craftsman...

Basil Dawkins[4], a prolific Jamaican playwright had this to say:

Arriving to study at the University of the West Indies, I was a certified Country Bumpkin. Part of the activity of freshman's week was that we all were required to attend a play at the Creative Arts Center on the Campus... I was told the play was called *Smile Orange*. I thought, *Smile Orange*, Lord spare me – *Smile Orange*? Not even Miss Vida's plays at the Methodist Church which I was forced to sit through when I was growing up had such stupid names as *Smile Orange*! Inside the Creative Arts Center now – and wow! Gush of cold air – it is air conditioned, you go in and the seats are soft – they are padded – this is good. I am tired, I am having doubts about this university thing, but now I am in an air-conditioned room in a soft chair and so as soon as this *Orange* thing starts, I will SLEEP!

Something magical happens that night in 1973. I had never seen an audience give a standing ovation. While I rubbed away the embarrassing goose pimples, standing and even bowing back to the actors was simply not enough I decide this *Smile Orange* thing is more than a laughing matter – and maybe a University education is not so bad after all.

The cast of *Smile Orange* changed often because the run was so long, but the classic cast was Grace McGhie, who created Miss Brandon, Carl Bradshaw, who became the epitome of Ringo, Stan Irons, the dangerous Joe, Vaughan Crosskill, the continually undermined Hotel Manager, and Glen Morrison, the lisping busboy.

It was just before this time in 1971 that I left Jamaica to follow a career in theatre in the UK, unfortunately missing this first famous production of *Smile Orange*. It was nearly four years before I once again directed at The Barn.

However, before my departure, my parents made it crystal clear I would be held responsible for what went on in their backyard in terms of presenting plays for public consumption. I had chosen to be thousands of miles away, but that was my decision, which did not, in their eyes, relieve me of my responsibility to them and to The Barn. Realising that if I chickened out of this obligation they would pull the plug on the theatre, I therefore hovered vaguely over the accounts and the running of the place from afar. I wasn't worried because Trevor was there. I knew he would continue to programme the productions for at least the next few years. He did. In 1973 two of his plays, which he directed himself, *Sleeper* and *Comic Strip* were presented on The Barn stage.

Pat Cumper,[5] a former Artistic Director of Talawa Theatre Company in the United Kingdom, a published playwright in her own right, writes:

My first clear memory of The Barn Theatre was going to see Trevor Rhone's popular comedy *Smile Orange*. A friend of mine, Harvel Peryer, was playing the bus boy and I remember Grace McGhie playing the much put-upon receptionist who was thinking about how best and on whom to bestow her "pearl".

Trevor Rhone was the drama teacher at my high school, the Queen's High School, and though I was never allowed by my mother to actually take part in any of the school's drama productions, I hung around them and did costumes and other tasks. After leaving school, my best friend, Cheryl Stuart, and I were invited by Trevor to be part of a series of improvisations he was using to write a play about relationships. It was eventually called *Comic Strip* and ran at The Barn where Cheryl and I played two young women sharing our first apartment. Playing one of the gentlemen who came and tried to seduce us was Carl Bradshaw, by then a bit of a star for his roles in *Smile Orange* and *The Harder They Come*. I remember being fined at my Leo club meeting for not being sufficiently indecent on stage, because I insisted on wearing a bra beneath the nightie and dressing gown I wore on stage for half of the play. I also remember delivering the cue for Carl to come on stage, looking to where he would stand before entering, to see, with horror, that he was not there. The Barn is a small theatre and I and most of the audience heard when Errol, who was running the show, left the lighting booth and ran around behind the theatre to the dressing rooms. We then heard, as we improvised madly and very badly, Carl and Errol come running back. Finally, Bradshaw was in place and so Cheryl and I redelivered the lines that were his cue to enter. Then we held our breaths as Carl stood laughing as we glanced at him panic stricken. He eventually strolled on and had the audience eating out of his hand in seconds, of course.

Carl was well known to like flirting and it occasionally, considering that Cheryl and I were barely nineteen at the time, became a little heavy handed. So we decided on a plan. The next time Carl came too close, we together reached towards his crotch and asked if we could please see what he was offering. He looked shocked, backed off and we got on like a house on fire after that.

In 1974, I paid what was meant to be a fleeting visit home to Jamaica. My work in Britain in the three year interim had begun to be reasonably rewarding, with professional acting roles and even one or two directorial credits under the belt. These included directing the first Jamaican pantomime to be produced in the UK, *Anansi and Brer Englishman*, under the auspices of fellow Jamaican, Frank Cousins, artistic director of the only black-led venue in London, the Dark and Light Theatre in Brixton.

It was a strange moment, this return in 1974. In my absence, much had taken place which I knew very little about and had had virtually no involvement in. I had seen neither *Sleeper* nor *Comic Strip* and *Smile Orange*. Nor had I any relationship with *See Mama*, *Sala* or *The Criminals*. I felt almost like a tourist. I was really enjoying the visitor treatment when Trevor, out of the blue, asked me to direct his latest play *School's Out*.

The idea of working at The Barn after a break of so many years in which I had been functioning as a professional director and actor in Britain, in such a different environment, filled me with misgiving. So much had taken place in my absence, I hardly recognized the place and was genuinely unsure of becoming involved once again. Ultimately, my carefully reasoned decision to direct *School's Out*, although set about with enormous doubt, once embarked upon, was never regretted.

I remember wondering at the time about the titles of the Rhone plays. S O, *Smile Orange*. S O, *School's Out* . He explained that after the success of *Smile Orange*, the notion came to him that the titles of his plays should all have an S. Hence *Schools Out*, *Sleeper*, *Comic Strip*. Others which appeared later on *One Stop Driver*, *Old Story Time*, *Bellas Gate Boy*, *Positive* also followed the rule. Only three of his plays did not comply. *The Gadget* written before *Smile Orange*, and which eventually became *Old Story Time* anyway, and *Two Can Play* and *The Game*.

In the process of preparing for work on *Schools Out*, the similarities of formula to *Smile Orange* were immediately apparent. In both plays there is only one setting (kitchen/ class room), a lead character whose name begun with R (Ringo and Roscoe, both rascals with glib tongues under which they concealed enterprise and revolt against the system). Joe in *Smile Orange* shares many character details with Joe in *Schools Out*, not only in name, because both characters are inward looking and ultimately dangerous. There are graphically similar titles (*Smile Orange*, *School's Out*); a single female character of dubious morality (Miss Brandon set on getting the best price for her "pearl", Mica set on getting the best deal for her higher class "pearl"); and they were very similar in length, and in using classic comedic routines (almost *commedia de'll artee*)[6] to highlight social situations in Jamaica. In *Smile Orange*, we witness the unpleasant aspects of tourism which brought out the worst and most exploitative side of those who served:

> Ringo: White people love to see black people bow down, you see!
> Joe: I will touch the ground if I can find a dollar bill down dere.
> Ringo: A will go further than dat, a will bury my head in di san'.

And Ringo will go even further, getting jobs for his "missis" two brothers as life guards, although he knows full well they can't swim and a tourist drowns as a result of their ineptitude.

Rhone's theory is that tourism should be like the orange of the title: a forbidden fruit. He makes this clear by highlighting the landowners quickness to capitalise on the well-known fear of young men, that of losing sexual potency; he puts out the story that slaves are better off not to eat oranges as they will "rotten out their balls". This kept the owners rich and the workers hungry. Tourism will rotten out the balls of the nation, especially those who serve the tourist: hungry for sexual excitement, greedily eating everything in sight. It is clear that trust and respect between fellow workers, community, even individual friendships, are victims when the culture of "dawg eat dawg" rules. In Jamaican parlance: "Di man fi di self"[7] being the order of the day. When his livelihood is threatened, Joe is quick to pull his knife on his fellow waiter.

In *School's Out*, Trevor was writing about a complex situation he knew so well, having learnt the mysteries of the staff room during his time as drama teacher at Melbourne School, housed amongst makeshift classrooms, imagined out of what was once the pavilion of the former Melbourne Cricket club. Here was Kingston College Junior School. Although there *were* classrooms of a sort, often teachers, especially the creative artists temporarily earning a meagre living teaching, preferred to be under the bleachers[8] where the real skill lay in dodging the sun as it moved, and finding the striped shadows. This was preferable to being in those hot overcrowded classrooms, with the constant sound of metal desks colliding with metal chairs, colliding with concrete floors. The students loved being led out of the oven-hot class rooms into the open air.

The staff room in *Schools Out* was not an exact carbon copy of the one at Melbourne, but it wasn't far off. When I returned home from the UK in 1965, Trevor actually convinced Mr. Douglas Forrest, then head master of Kingston College, to allow me to join the staff of this highly regarded school. I was a qualified teacher after all. It was a privilege to join that staff. It was bulging with talent. Among others, the teachers included Maud Fuller, Rachel Manley,[9] Trevor Parchment, Marjorie Whylie,[10] and of course Trevor Rhone. The students were particularly lucky that year to have these talented Jamaicans as their teachers for a while. However, the smelly staff room was much too small to accommodate this number of staff. I, for one, never had a designated work place, having to "cotch" apologetically at a corner of the central table, in the seat nearest the toilet.

There was the occasional lazy teacher, yes, but most memorable was the staff toilet, more often than not, out of order. The raw material for *Schools Out* was all there. It just needed a Rhone, first to recognize the dramatic potential, and then to pull it together. This he did brilliantly, adding the racial element and exaggerating the loud vulgarity of Roscoe, the wasted talent. Sadly, the template for the character Hopal Hendry, "the half-educated, ungrammatical, conspicuously under-qualified teacher" did exist fully blown in the Melbourne staff room.

In the play, a near riot in the school canteen has been quelled by the use of violent intervention by one of the staff members, leaving a student with a bloody nose. Mica enters the staff room:

MICA: Oh Mr. Hendry, there is a message for you from Mr. Dacres. He says you may now come for your lunch.
HENDRY: I am not hungry. (*Very angrily*)
ROSCO: I hungry bad. (*He points Hendry towards the canteen*) Put it on mi bill, don't forget. (*Hendry is on his way to towards the canteen when the bell goes. He stops and returns to his desk*) What happen?
HENDRY: The bell ring.
ROSCO: I never hear it, man.
HENDRY: I have a class. (*Collects his books and goes out in the direction away from the canteen*).
ROSCO: Is a good thing I'm not hungry. I better check if I have a class. (*He does*). I have a class, yes. I going to eat.[11]

By exaggerating the absence of industry in the staff room, the staff's faint interest in the education of the students, Rhone drives home his political point: the inescapable need for a complete overhaul of Jamaica's education system.

Once again, as in *Smile Orange*, the Rhone dialogue being so precise, audience recognition was immediate and their reaction expansive. *Schools Out* is, arguably, the better of these two socially conscious plays; the construction is more seamless, but splitting of hairs may not be necessary here.

Casting as always was crucial. Oliver Samuels[12] was, if I remember correctly, acting in an Italian classic, Goldoni's *Servant of Two Masters*, at the time. My friend and tutor, Wycliffe Bennett, had directed him in it. He was sensational. I determined to have him as my Roscoe.

Oliver's first memory of The Barn was going there to see Trevor Rhone's *Smile Orange*:

> I was amazed to discover that the space was transformed from a garage to a theatre space. I had this yearning for wanting to perform in that space. Opportunity came when I was cast in Trevor's next new work *School's Out*. I first heard the phrase, "a work in progress", at The Barn. Came about after the play was read and the director, Yvonne Jones Brewster, was not happy with some aspects of the content and structure of the play. She said, "Let us view this piece as a work in progress", and decided she would have a discussion with the writer. Of course, changes were made and they went into rehearsals in earnest. I learnt so much from Yvonne's directorial skills and *School's Out* became at the time one of Jamaica's most successful plays.
>
> In the play a very eager young man, Vernon Darby, was cast. He was fresh from the country and spoke with a very strange country accent. This accent did not fit in with the rhythm of the other actors and no matter how hard the director tried to get him to speak like us, it just sounded off beat. It became very frustrating to the other actors and the director. One day she just exclaimed: "Oliver, see if you can help him to talk." Vernon and I worked on the speech patterns and he did so well that he won Best Supporting Actor in the JCDC[13] awards that year

I believe this was Oliver's first foray into the local dialect on the Jamaican stage, and the rest is history, as they say. Oliver Samuels has been treading the boards without ceasing since then. He has become an iconic presence on stage, on Television, on video and is well known to audiences in the United States, Canada and the United Kingdom, where a play with Oliver is almost a dead cert for the management to dust off the sold out signs. His timing is legendary, and although his prowess at delivering well-aimed cannon balls of dialogue is what we have come to expect, he can produce excellent sensitive portrayals, such as the father to Lennie Henry's *Chef* on

British TV. Perhaps we make the mistake of undervaluing Samuels because he is so funny.

The work of Louise Bennett, Bob Marley, Usain Bolt, Marcus Garvey carry the Jamaican flag proudly in the world. In theatre, I boldly venture to say Oliver Samuels does the same.

The production of *School's Out* benefited from having not only an excellent script and set, but thrived on the quality and talent that all members of the cast brought to it. The lovely Pauline Cowan (soon to be Kerr) as Mica the only female in this Godforsaken staff room; Vin McKie, idly strumming his guitar in lieu of ever leaving his seat; Calvin Foster's reverend gentleman must take the prize for the most loathsome creep; Bobb Kerr's leering Scotsman... Oliver has mentioned Vernon Derby, whose indomitable scorpion, quick-to-protect-his-back characterization of Hopal Hendry was superb. Harold Brady, Trevor Rhone and Trevor Nairne alternating in all presenting suitably slimy Russ Dacres (Crusader, get it?). We were lucky, too, with a very-new-to-theatre Brian Heap and Glen Campbell, who were also members of the alternating cast. I think this is one of the most creative, cohesive casts I had worked with anywhere, up until that moment. I enjoyed the process and I hope they did too.

I soon returned to my work in England, but Trevor and I did not lose touch. Trevor's letters, always poetic but hugely political, kept our long distance friendship fuelled. I was sometimes able to anticipate from them what the next play would be about... For example:

> '... been meaning to share the story of a mentally ill man who threatened to jump from the fourth floor of the Kingston Public Hospital. Very soon a crowd gathered to watch the spectacle. You may be thinking that those gathered would be concerned about the man's well-being. No Mrs Brewster. Instead, a chant of encouragement went up 'Jump Jump Jump'. The man jumped and was impaled on sharpened steel – atop the concrete security wall. He survived. The crowd left somewhat dissatisfied at the turn of events in the afternoon's blood sports. Yesterday was Emancipation day here.

Did Trevor's *Everyman* come out of this?

By now (it is 1975), the closely knit trio of Munair, Trevor and Yvonne had, to all intents and purposes, slipped into oblivion. The success of Trevor as a mature playwright, especially with *Smile Orange* and *Schools Out* to his credit, had made him financially secure. The Barn was not a place where one could easily make vast sums of money. Understandably he explored other options. I, too, having all but abandoned working in Jamaica, choosing to concentrate on my theatrical career in England, was doing reasonably well.

Trevor went on to write a number of plays after *School's Out,* but it was eight years, in 1982, before another Trevor Rhone play, *Two Can Play*, was seen at The Barn. A fine example of a two-hander, with all the makings of a classic, sensitively exploring the close relationship between man and wife. It also addresses the politically unstable nature of the Jamaican economy, which forced citizens to look for the almighty US dollar in any place possible, and probably impossible.

This play had a tremendous impact on other Jamaican playwright/ producers. The catch-phrase was: "Rhone says Two Can Play but he also knows two can pay."

As time went by, with very few exceptions, playwrights became producers of their own work. It's interesting that this almost Shakespearean model reappeared four hundred years later in the small island of Jamaica. Any analysis of performed Jamaican plays will reveal the phenomenon of writers producing their own work. In looking at the plays produced at The Barn, after the first five years when the theatre produced all the work, one would be hard pressed to find many new Jamaican plays which were not also produced and sometimes directed by the playwright, not to mention acted in. The budding playwright-producer-actor-director that the system was encouraging, soon learned the art and necessity, to be fair, of keeping the financial bottom line in close perspective.

Trevor Rhone had a deep understanding and perhaps appreciation of the feminine psyche. In some of the female roles, the protagonists are complicated, difficult women to love. In *Yes Mama*, the mother in question is in the business of exploiting her daughter's saleable assets for profit. We are allowed to recognise, if not sympathise with, the mother's dilemma, which determines her reprehensible actions.

In *Smile Orange*, his portrayal of Miss Brandon made uncomfortable viewing for women with feminist values, as she could be seen as the antithesis of all they stood for. But Miss Brandon, who is in one of the dead-end jobs in the hotel industry, can be forgiven for thinking that the grass must be greener in the United States, even if it means she has to offer herself cheaply to a "one legged tourist man". Although, when he runs out – make that limps out – on her, she is only getting what she deserves, there always lurks a sneaking sympathy for her. To keep the job she must ultimately rely on, she is obliged to continue speaking in a fake American accent as she answers the phone and addresses guests. As the curtain comes down, we suspect she most probably will be on an even sharper lookout for the next viable escape opportunity.

Mica, in *School's Out*, is quite difficult to like as she is clearly of the opinion that the white teacher is a superior being to all the black men in the staff room, when he is obviously even more flawed than they are. The "whiteness is rightness" conviction rears its ugly head. The society appears to agree that the white teacher is the man with a future. Once again, the woman's choices are thin on the ground, so we appreciate her predicament.

In *Two Can Play*, his portrayal of Gloria is perhaps more three dimensional. We are allowed to enter into her most private moments with profound delicacy; in her interplay with Jim she again is full-bodied in her representation. Two-handed plays are notoriously difficult to pull off successfully, but this is a shining example of the genre. As a writer of comedies, Rhone is often the master of seeing the ridiculous side of what, in other hands, may have become a deeply dramatic tragedy or even melodramatic. In *Two Can Play*, he is on top form. He does not ridicule Jim, the husband who sends his wife alone and unprotected into the entrails of Uncle Sam's seamier underbelly, but makes him tolerably likeable, while we appreciate Gloria, the intrepid wife, as a fine example of the cunning thoughtful, resourceful Jamaican female. Perhaps a small point of criticism, which I have heard expressed by others and to which I subscribe: the ending. Gloria may be just a touch too submissive to allow continuing belief in the character she has so successfully maintained throughout the play.

In 1988, Rhone co-authored a revue, *One Stop Driver*, with Louis Marriott (1935-2016) a playwright, broadcaster and historian.[14] Here is Louis's recollection of the collaboration:

> In 1988, Rhone and Hyatt invited me to join them to complete a triumvirate of friends and colleagues with a long association in theatre to stage a musical revue at The Barn. We agreed that Trevor and I would share the scriptwriting, Charlie would direct, and all three would be co-producers. Over differences regarding sponsorship issues, I resigned as co-producer, so a "Rhone-Hyatt-Marriott" production became a "Rhone-Hyatt" production, although I continued with my share of production work. Then, shortly before opening night, differences over the product emerged. Charlie was replaced as director by Trevor and I wrote a news release to the effect that Charlie had resigned as director because his workload as Entertainment Editor of the new *Jamaica Record* newspaper would not afford him the time to continue as Director.

Successful collaboration was never a big feature of Trevor Rhone's career.

In 1992, Trevor Nairne directed the 21st anniversary production of *Smile Orange*. This example of tribute from one senior Jamaican theatre person to another does not occur as often as perhaps it might and merits comment.

In 1999, *Old Story Time*, the rewrite of *The Gadget,* which had first been staged in 1979 at the Way Out theatre at the Jamaica Pegasus, was finally given a showing at The Barn, when perhaps its audience pulling-power might have peaked.

Old Story Time is a favourite with many Jamaicans at home and abroad. Trevor admitted to me once, long ago, that he thought of it as his favourite play. Another of our heated discussions evolved, as it is certainly not first on *my* list of favourite Rhone works, perhaps because of the overly contrived style of storytelling, which, to my mind, ultimately undermine the pathos. I have always been in a minority of perhaps one on this.

Yvonne and Trevor

On one of my annual visits to the island, Trevor showed me the unpublished manuscript of the first half of an autobiography he had embarked upon. He had been invited to read an excerpt from it at Calabash, the Jamaican literary festival, brain child of Kwame Dawes, Colin Channer and Justine Henzell. He was quite chuffed at the success it had enjoyed. It quickly seemed to me to have the makings of a one-man show. Trevor had been planning to do readings from the text, using a lectern, as part of his repertoire on his many visits to university campuses in the United States. After working on this project for a while, it struck me that it would make a wonderful one-person show which he, Trevor, could *perform*. Valerie Chuck, one-time administrator at The Barn, recalled this in an interview in 2016:

In 2002, Trevor asked Yvonne to direct him in a rehearsed reading of the first half of his autobiography *Bellas Gate Boy*. He had read an excerpt of it at Calabash, the lively literary festival on the south coast of Jamaica, which had gone down so well he thought he might get it produced and directed as something to present on his many trips abroad. With one thing and another, Yvonne prepared a draft script and before long she was in Jamaica and the one man play was in rehearsal. Of course the script was far from perfect, needing a multitude of cuts and reconfigurations during the rehearsal process. They both understood that this would be a kind of swan song. On the other hand it brought back some memories of when they were young!

Warming to the idea, Trevor was anxious for it to happen. He seemed quite taken with the idea of the dramatization and told me to get on with it: "...if it works, Brewster, we can do one last show at The Barn with you directing and me acting".

I did get on with it and promptly adapted the manuscript for the stage. The Barn Production of *Bellas Gate Boy*, with Trevor playing the lead, alternating with the talented Alwyn Scott, opened in the dying days of December 2002.

The small theatre was once again, after an intermission of some twenty-eight years, host to the final collaboration between the two old war horses. It was a strange and rather surreal experience as we struggled to come to terms with the text, not to mention the time-eroded texture of the relationship. Alwyn Scott was excellent and received the award as that year's best actor in the Actor Boy Awards for his portrayal of the young Rhone. We rehearsed in the mornings with Nicky Brown, then new to Stage Management but now Jamaican administrative theatrical eminence gris, in charge of us. She learned very quickly to be a very strict controller of us two, who rather preferred reminiscing to rehearsing. It was a sad and a glad event as Trevor and I both knew in our hearts that The Barn did not have much longer to survive; the writing was on the wall which read that The Barn was too small and weak a player to defend itself against the might of the KSAC (the Kingston and St Andrew Corporation) and more importantly changing public taste. Alwyn Scott recalls:[15]

Bellas Gate Boy, my third production at The Barn, was my first ever one-man project. I did this only because you believed I had the capacity. I was honoured by the time and effort put in to make the interpretation of the role my own and not a replica of Trevor's version. I got then how important it is to be honest to oneself and to the character. And then there were the stories you and Trevor shared with me of that "womb" for our indigenous theatre – The Barn. Those stories deserve to be shared.

In 2005, the final year of the existence of The Barn, Trevor wrote an issue-based educative work for the Ministry of Health: *Positive*, a cautionary tale relating to the spread of Aids. Efficiently directed by Fabian Thomas and fit for the purpose of health education, the production sported a large cast led by the senior female actor, Dorothy Cunningham. But in truth, this had no relationship to The Barn. Trevor's close involvement had ended long ago, as any cursory analysis of his relationship with The Barn will show. Above all, it was the success of *Smile Orange* which had the greatest influence on his day-to-day commitment to The Barn as an experimental venue primarily dedicated to housing his early work. The theatre by that time had been extended to seat more people, one hundred and forty-four, when packed like sardines, but larger venues meant more income, a wider audience and, as far as he was concerned, brought him personally nearer to the Theatre 77 aim of professional theatre in twelve years. Here he was, after only half the time, six years, almost earning a living from his writing, and not only him, but some of the actors and technicians as well.

This was the time when the ties that bound the closely knit trio of Munair, Trevor and myself begun to loosen their hold. Writing is a solitary pursuit, and Trevor accordingly withdrew from the coal-face of the mundane matter of the management of The Barn project. Munair was anxious to test his wings in areas of theatre other than acting, and began exploring directing opportunities and gained valuable experience in other media. I too had been restless to rediscover what I could achieve in the UK, and had left Jamaica and The Barn behind in mid 1971. The trio still operated well to all intents and purposes, but something organic, something fundamental, changed with the success of *Smile Orange*.

After mounting *School's Out*, Trevor began producing most of his plays elsewhere. He worked, with Dennis Scott directing, on his Jamaican version of *Everyman*, which was presented at LTM'S Little Theatre and wrote a pantomime, *Music Boy*, for the LTM, among many works authored by him and presented elsewhere, but this small book has concerned itself solely with productions which took place at The Barn theatre.

I regard the four year period between the production of the *Gadget* 1970, *Smile Orange* (1971), *Sleeper* (1971) and *Comic Strip* (1973) and *School's Out* (1974) as the pinnacle of Trevor's creative epoch in theatre. To have written five plays in just under four years, two of which have become undisputed classics of Jamaican theatre, was a gargantuan achievement.

"Trevor", I once asked, "why write plays?" His response:

The objective of my plays is to mirror the lives of the ordinary man, to reaffirm his strengths in such a way that he learns to diminish his weaknesses and to believe that he can make a positive difference in his society.

Endnotes

1. Ancile Gloudun, actor and producer, began in the UCWI drama group, joined the New Theatre Group, and appeared in the films, *Piranha II* and *The Wide Sargasso Sea*. See *The Jamaican Theatre, Highlights...*, p. 276.

2. Keith "Ginger" Knight's play *Underwriters, Undercover* played at The Barn in April 2004. Previously in 2002 his *Part Time Lover* had been presented. Ginger Knight is a pioneer of "roots" theatre. His plays include *Boy Blue, Dis-A-Reggae, Don-Man, Gilbert, Higglers, Poly-triks*. His most famous play, *Whiplash* (1982) was published in *3 Jamaican Plays: A Postcolonial Anthology*, ed. Honor Ford Smith (Paul Issa, 2011). More recent work includes *The Tiger Squad* and *Kung Fu Cowboy*. His comedy *Room for Rent* became a film in 2005. See Cecilia Campbell-Livingston, "Ginger Knight Heads to the Movies", *Jamaica Observer*, 27 July, 2014.

3. *Two Can Play and School's Out* (Longman, 1986).

4. Basil Dawkins, actor and playwright. After UWI he became a member of the Caribbean Theatre Workshop. His plays include, *Flatmate, Parson and Mrs Jones, Couple, Champagne and Sky Juice, Same Song Different Tune, God Bless, Power Play, Toy Boy, Feminine Justice, What The Hell is Happening to Us, Dear?, No Dirty Money, A Gift for Mom, No Disrespect, Hot Spot, Uptown Bangarang I & II, Which Way is Out?* His *Hot Spot* was published in the Heinemann Caribbean Writers Series. See *The Jamaican Theatre. Highlights...*, p. 265

5. Pat Cumper wrote and produced over a dozen plays whilst still working in Jamaica. They include *The Rapist, Benny's Song.* In the UK she has worked with the Talawa Theatre Company (as Artistic Director 2006-2012), Carib Theatre Company, The Royal Court, Blue Mountain Theatre, BBC Radio 4. Her radio series *One Bright Child* won the CRE radio award. Her collection of plays, *Inner Yardie: Three Plays* was published by Peepal Tree in 2014.

6. Commedia de'll arte: Rosco/Ringo: Harlequin: Mica/Miss Brandon,

Columbine: Joe/Joe, Il Dottore: Hopal/Bus Boy, Pierro: Chaplin/ Dacres: Il Capitano?.

7. Di man fi di self: every man for himself.

8. Bleachers are the bench-like uncovered seating which surrounded the cricket pitch. Melbourne had once been a formal cricket ground.

9. Rachel Manley is a poet and memoirist, famous for her sequence of books around the Manley family: *Drumblair* (1996), *Slipstream: A Daughter Remembers* (2000), *In My Father's Shadow* (2004) and *Horses in Her Hair* (2009). Peepal Tree published her second poetry collection, *A Light Left On* in 1991.

10. Marjorie Whylie (1944-) is a musician and musicologist who worked with Louise Bennett on Jamaican pantomimes. She was Musical Director of the National Dance Theatre Company for 45 years. She was awarded a Bronze Musgrave. See Richard Johnson, "Marjorie Whylie's Curtain Call", *Jamaica Observer*, 9 April 2013.

11. *Old Story Time and Other Plays* (Essex: Longman, 1981) p. 127.

12. Oliver Samuels (1948-), perhaps the most popular of all Jamaican comedians, with his alter ego Olivius Adams in *Oliver at Large*. He played in the film *Countryman* (1982) and co-starred with Lenny Henry in the TV series, *Chef* (1993-1996).

13. Jamaica Cultural Development Commission.

14. Louis Marriott (1935-2016). His plays (at least 23 in all) included *The Shepherd, Bedward, Office Chase, A Pack of Jokers* and *Playboy*. See *The Gleaner*, "Louis Marriott Dies", 3 Aug. 2016.

15. Alwyn Scott (1960-) Jamaica's leading classical actor, winner of numerous awards in leading roles.

CHAPTER SEVEN: MUNAIR'S BARN, 1974-1977

Aficionados of theatre, local and international, have from time to time wondered why we did not open the field to other young Jamaican playwrights instead of always waiting for Trevor to come up with the goods, a practice which led to the need to fill the stage with a variety of foreign product? In hindsight this is a very good question, but back then we were not really concerned.

However, in 1972 Munair did exactly that when he commissioned, directed and produced and the play, *See Mama* by Edward E. Henry.

Munair tells his own story :

> I began to widen my skill base. I facilitated, and stage managed one of the few international touring shows The Barn hosted, Dem Two, with two Guyanese actors, Ken Corsbie and Marc Matthews. By 1971, I was getting into the swing of becoming a truly all purpose theatre man. *See Mama* turned me into a producer/ director.
>
> After the play's success there was no hope for me. I was a theatre person whether I liked it on not!

Munair recognized the potential of *See Mama*, a biographical piece written by Edward Henry, an expatriate Jamaican living in the United States. He facilitated the creation of the piece at The Barn. This was Munair's first attempt at producing and his third at directing. *See Mama*, opening in late December 1971, after Trevor had decided to present his megahit *Smile Orange* at larger venues, ran for three months and clocked up 58 performances.

Munair likes the story of how Stafford (Harrison) Ashani[1] would make his entrance on a motorbike every night riding from the corner of Oxford and Norwood Roads which bordered the venue. The audience would hear the bike coming from in the distance, and end up right in the auditorium. After shutting it off and leaning it up by the side, Stafford would then disappear round the back and then reappear up on stage for the scene.

Stafford could also apparently "cry living eye-water" at a certain moment in the play every night – every time – and the backstage people would take bets at every show as to whether he'd cry for real each time. Stafford, competent and complete man of theatre even then, also designed the set; no matter that the front flat almost fell over onto the audience one night and the first row people had to quickly stand up and catch it before havoc was wreaked.

With that experience under his belt in 1974, Munair stepped into the breach, the vacuum created by an over-committed Trevor – who one must not forget was still teaching, doing radio commercials, writing other work. Added to which, absentee landlord Yvonne was away in England, working. With the unstinting help of George Silvera and Gladstone Murray, Munair became the "main man" of the place for a while.

After *School's Out* closed its doors, Munair really took on the mantle as arbiter (artistic director if you like, even though this term was never ever used at The Barn in all of its forty years of existence) of what went on the stage of The Barn Theatre for a number of very important years. One of his talents is his ability and desire to introduce new talent, as he had demonstrated with *Ask Mama*.

Munair began to take chances. A big risky one was *The Criminals*[2] by the celebrated Cuban writer Jose Triana, a theatrical *tour de force* which he produced, designed, and directed. His friend and colleague Stafford Ashani was to a large extent the instigator and supporter of the production of this piece, by insisting that it was potentially an opportunity for presenting theatre of the highest order, and so it was. The play, using the art of role-playing, which takes place between three siblings, is a powerful theatrical vehicle.

Munair knew it would not prove commercial and it ended up playing to houses of thirty people on average each night for about a month or so. But in the end all the actors – Anna Hearne, Hilary Nicholson, and Stafford himself – all revelled and excelled in their roles. Those who saw it consider it one of Munair Zacca's best directorial efforts.

Hilary Nicholson remembers:

I appeared at The Barn in 1974 in *The Criminals*. It was very hard to do; not sure I ever fully understood it! Stafford was in it. I wanted very much to do it but felt inexperienced and insecure as an actor. I do remember the feeling that Stafford seemed so much more competent and confident than me!

Munair adds:

After *The Criminals* other serious playwrights came to me with work:

Carmen Tipling asked me to direct her first play, *Straight Man*, which she produced. I will leave it to Carmen to say how she thought it went!

Carmen Tipling herself recalls:

My first encounter with The Barn was during a visit to Jamaica, during the late 1960s... while living in California, USA, when I saw a production of *Ask Your Mama* by Langston Hughes. The context and ambience of The Barn Theatre, the then Theatre 77, the performance, as well as the enthusiasm of the players, convinced me that I should be associated with this theatre. And, many years later, my plays were showcased at The Barn.

Carmen Tipling's *Straight Man* played at The Barn in 1974.[3] Two years later, in 1976, so did her second play *Skeleton Inside*. Both of these plays were Bronze Medal winners in the Playwriting category of the Jamaica Festival Literary Competition. Having returned home from California, USA, where she had among other things worked as a script researcher at Warner Bros Studios, she soon became a force to be reckoned with in many fields of endeavour, including spells as a leading public relations guru and Special Assistant to Minister of Industry and Tourism, P.J. Patterson, who was later Minister of Foreign Affairs and Prime Minister of Jamaica.

Straight Man was the first Jamaican play to chronicle the plight of Jamaican nationals in North America, those who were not legitimate migrants, did not have Green Cards, or were *bona fide* farm workers. The play demonstrated the changes that some nationals, who did not have visas or other legitimate papers, and were therefore not "not straight", had to go through to follow their American dream. The production boasted for the most part mesmerizing performances. The title role was played by American, Bob Morris. The leads were Stafford (Harrison) Ashani, Christine Bell, Ruel Cooke. Arthur Brown completed the cast of *Straight Man*
Munair has this memory of the performance:

Theatre is often about what goes on backstage out of sight of the audience, but in this production Arthur Brown (the father of Dennis Brown, the late singer) was possibly inebriated and having forgotten his lines, dried on stage and was unable to continue for what seemed an eternity. Eventually, I apologized and said that there were two possibilities: either that I'd discontinue the show and give them back their money, or, we could continue with me reading in the part, and they unanimously chose that I read in the part, and so I did.

Carmen gives her own account of her next play:

The Skeleton Inside examined being a Jamaican and being prepared to stay in the country and build it, when it wasn't popular to be a Jamaican, much less to stay in this country, or even attempt to build in the decade of the 70s.

This play was directed by Dennis Scott, one of country's leading dancers, poet, playwright, director and a teacher, who was the Principal of the then Jamaica School of Drama and later went on to make history at the School of Drama, at Yale University in the USA. Dennis saw *The Skeleton Inside* as a paean to a developing society still struggling to find its way, after some 14 years as an independent nation.

Some members of the cast are of Jamaican legend: Grace McGhie, Honor Ford Smith, Pauline Cowan, and Trevor Nairne, who is perhaps better known for his prowess as director. And there were many first timers, who turned in memorable performances, such as Jonathan Brown, Val Morris, Howard Facey, Pat Lindsay, Cecile Clayton, and Zac Henry.

Both of these plays established Carmen's playwriting skills, and her willingness to take on subjects that are not necessarily easy to confront, either in real life, or on stage. After the production of these two important plays, Carmen Tipling did not desert the theatre entirely. She later teamed up with the late Ted Dwyer to write the rollicking pantomime, *Bruckings* and the multi-award winning musical, the spectacular *Arawak Gold*. Today, her skill and work as a sensitive serious Jamaican playwright is greatly missed.

Munair's taste and ideas continued to enjoy a free reign. His next directorial outing, which he also produced, was again a new play and the first piece of work written by his colleague associate and friend the gifted Stafford Ashani, who went on to became a theatrical powerhouse in Jamaica, until his untimely death in 2009. I knew Stafford Harrison as he had been one of my students at Excelsior High School where I had taught Drama. He, even then, showed early signs of the innovative and restless artist he was to become. Munair Zacca enjoyed an interesting relationship with Stafford, although two more different people it is hard to imagine.

Munair recalls:

I knew Stafford for almost forty years. I first met him when he and I were cast in a play called *A Liberated Woman* written by Barry Reckord. This was around 1971 and Stafford was still a student at Excelsior High School at the time and Victor, his father, actually reminded me that Stafford had to get permission from the school to be in the production, especially since the play was of a somewhat adult nature.[4] We became the best of friends, and eventually went on to work on several productions together for many many years.

Munair produced Ashani's *The Quickie* (1976), which drew on Ashani's experience of running a candy business, which had exposed him to the rampant chicanery of the business world. It was a fitting prelude to his more ambitious work, *Masqueraders* (1977).

Members of cast in plays at The Barn more often than not, had important day jobs. Casts were paid something, but with such a tiny auditorium and possibly playing for only four nights a week the sum was often not a large one. Not "giving up the day job" had a vibrant meaning at The Barn. For instance, one of the leading psychiatrists in Jamaica, Aggrey Irons, was a cast member of *The Quickie*, as had been public relations high-flyer, Christine Bell, in *Straight Man*.

Stafford Ashani and Munair Zacca's actively creative relationship ran deep. It is thought that Munair Zacca was the prototype for the character of Mad Dog in *Masqueraders*, one of whose speeches (as spoken by Mad Dog's alter ego Heirstone) reads:

> ...Our audience isn't ready for that sort of thing (a play without a script) they're narrow minded and complacent. They want to laugh, poke jokes at the same old cornball falling down on the slippery banana peel. They want to burst their sides, not think. They've had a long week at the office and they come to be entertained.

Soon after *The Quickie*, Munair directed *Sweet Talk* by Guyanese playwright Michael Abbensetts[5] for Lloyd Reckord's National Theatre Trust, which was meant to be presented at the Creative Arts Centre at UWI Mona. This had to close prematurely. In fact it never opened because of some administrative oversight to do with obtaining the rights. Frustrated, Munair then decided not only to produce and direct the work at The Barn but to play the supporting role of Dennis. Apparently, I donated $500 J towards mounting this production, so as to make up for Munair's disappointment at having the production at UWI cancelled so suddenly.

Again Munair Zacca seized opportunities when they presented themselves, and with some style managed to snatch success out of the mouth of disaster. The cast of *Sweet Talk* was strong, including Honor Ford Smith and Hilary Nicholson. Michael Abbensetts was soon to enjoy great success as writer of the first black British television series, *Empire Road* among many other theatre successes, but there is a school of thought that argues that *Sweet Talk* is his most enduring play for the theatre, even though it was his first. As a relative newcomer to the London scene, having arrived there fresh from studying in Canada, he witnessed at first hand the huge waste of Caribbean talent due to what was then called colour prejudice, not racism. This quite shocked his sensibilities and *Sweet Talk* was a result of that outrage. It was a personal thing, too, as he used a cousin's lifestyle dilemmas as the template for the lead character.

The period between 1974 and 1977 was a very productive era when Munair was "in virtual artistic charge" of The Barn. Unfortunately, this came to an end with the closing of the production of *Sweet Talk* in 1977. Munair became busy with other production outfits, with Jamaican Television; he is still regularly seen on screen in locally produced programmes.

As far as his association with The Barn goes, he disappeared from sight for nearly a decade and was next seen on that tiny stage in *The Game* by Trevor Rhone in 1985. It may be of interest to note that this play was only the second Trevor Rhone play to be presented at The Barn since *Schools Out* in 1974. So at least two members of the original trio reunited in 1985.

Some three years later, in 1988, Munair again joined forces with Trevor (and Louis Marriott who co-authored), in the light-hearted, revue-inspired *One Stop Driver*. After that, it was another fourteen years before Munair was seen on The Barn stage when, in March 1994 to be exact, he tried his hand at writing a three hander called *Play It*, which he also produced, directed, and played the lead in. I think this exercise probably made him reconsider his position. Perhaps he decided writing was not for him.

Munair Zacca appeared at The Barn on four more occasions – which demonstrated his versatility – before it closed its doors in 2005. In 1995, he was directed by Pablo Hoilett in a popular revue *Jamaica Rundown*, written by Aston Cooke. In the following year he appeared in *Puppy Love* by Patrick Brown, directed by Trevor Nairne. 1999, saw him appear in David Heron's *Against His Will*, and finally in 2001, he appeared in Basil Dawkins' third production of his tried and tested *Couples*.

Having played such an important and pivotal role in the development of this tiny theatre, here is how Munair attempts to recall in a letter to me, the first far-off days when he was introduced to the wonders of theatre:

> I can't remember whether I met you or Trevor first, but I do recall that you and I met at a party and spent pretty much the whole time talking about acting and the theatre, and you relating to me your experiences at Rose Bruford, including the time when as a student you had the privilege and treat of going to see Laurence Olivier rehearse *Coriolanus*, as I listened to everything in awe.

Up to that point, I had never set my foot upon a stage outside of High School at Jamaica College, but had deep longings and aspirations to be an actor.

I also recall striking up a close friendship with Trevor; him giving me voice lessons in exchange for me giving him driving lessons... Remember I drove you back from Ocho Rios in the wee hours of one morning in your red, or was it white, MGB? We had gone to see Eartha Kitt perform and for you to interview her... You were with RJR [Real Jamaica Radio] at the time. Youth!

One Love to Munair.

Endnotes

1. Stafford (Harrison) Ashani (1953-2009) studied film at New York University. As managing director of A Plus Video Production in Jamaica he was responsible for producing music videos and concert recordings for a variety of reggae stars. His plays include *The Quickie, Masqueraders, Anancy and the Unsung Heroes Out West, Foreign Mind* and *Bar Jonah*. For a more extensive bio and interview, see *Visions and Voices*, pp. 111-132.
2. Jose Triana (1931-) *La Noche de los asesinos* (1965) won the Casas de las Americas Prize in 1966. It was also translated as *The Night of the Assassins*.
3. Carmen Tipling (1943-) grew up in Kingston, studied for her degree in the USA and worked as a motion picture and TV researcher for Warner Bros. In Jamaica she was director of Communications Consultants for 20 years then worked with the state Jamaican Information Service. Her plays include *During Lunch They Had a Revolution, Skeleton Inside!* and *Stowaway*. See *Visions and Voices* for a more extensive bio and an interview, pp. 282-303.
4. In *A Liberated Woman* the leading actress spent a considerable time in the nude.
5. Michael Abbensetts (1938-2016) was born in Guyana, educated there and in Canada, and settled in the UK from the early 1960s. His first play, *Sweet Talk* appeared in 1973. Thereafter he mainly worked in television with *The Museum Attendant, Inner City Blues, Crime and Passion, Black Christmas, Alterations, Samba, The Dark House, In the Mood, Easy Money, Outlaw, Eldorado, Big George is Dead, Living Together*. He reached his biggest audience with the first black soap opera in the UK, *Empire Road* (1978-79). See *Visions and Voices* for a more extensive bio and an interview, pp. 28-45.

CHAPTER EIGHT: BEHIND THE SCENES

All ventures, however small, require coherent maintenance, management and administration: someone eventually has to take ultimate formal responsibility.

My day-to-day involvement with The Barn theatre had virtually come to an end in 1971. It was never fully revived to be honest. I was now resident in the UK. Yet, I was continually made to understand, in no uncertain terms, that I was the person who remained responsible and answerable to my parents, who owned the property, for the day-to-day running of the place. Their primary concern was not so much with cultural or artistic values. They left that to others, but wanted to be assured that the laws of the land, with regard to libel and obscenity, were not flouted on their property.

This overseeing requirement was extremely difficult to achieve successfully from a distance of so many thousands of miles. I was also meant to have the last word in what went on artistically… in theory anyway. At first, scripts used to arrive in London for me to vet, but this practice did not last very long. Mail between Jamaica and the UK took an inordinate amount of time to arrive; it still does. Of course, there was no internet down which scripts could travel in seconds, so I found it virtually impossible to judge what would be right for The Barn audience from so far away.

It was no good asking Trevor, who was busy with the administration of the *Smile Orange* product among many other things, and Munair had more than enough on his plate to even contemplate taking on this extra burden.

However, someone had to take ultimate responsibility. In the interim, Gladstone Murray stepped into the breach. Mr. Murray, as he was known, was one of my father's chain men, plain Murray to some, but always Mr. Murray to those who knew what lay behind the inscrutable face. My father was a land surveyor, and in those days one had to hold the chain so that the old fashioned theodolite could read the distances between poles etc. Hence chain man. Mr. Murray became the caretaker of The Barn in the deepest sense of the word, gradually capturing the operation of the bar and eventually graduating to handling the accounts on my behalf. He became the local guardian of the finances and ruled backstage with a rod of iron. It was he who posted the proposed scripts to me in London.

I am therefore forever grateful to Gladstone Murray for being my faithful agent for so many years. This is what I wrote when he died on 4 September 2010:

> Gladstone Murray was born on 8th March 1923 in Hampton, St. Ann. I have known him since I was a little girl of nearly seven, when I vaguely remember my Uncle Alvin coming home from the war in Europe in late 1945 and I can see Mr. Murray in my mind's eye there to greet him, standing straight and proud.
>
> Mr. Murray worked for my family for at least five decades… at first as my father's chainman – my father was a land surveyor and an important part of getting the measurements accurate in those long-off days was the skill in holding the long metal chain in exactly the correct position. Chainmen ruled before the computer.
>
> Mr. Murray ruled!

My personal tribute to this man must, though, centre on his dedication to The Barn Theatre… to theatre in Jamaica… and to me, by extension. For many years, many more than one would imagine, my solitary bank account in Jamaica was one on which Mr. Murray was the only other signatory. For years he would collect the rentals and look after The Barn on my behalf. I often tell the story of once when I was on my annual visit and we were having our catch-up meeting under the mango tree, he presented the blue school exercise book with all the transactions scribbled in, with this comment:

> GM: Too much money in the account you know Miss Von, so I opened a CD.
>
> YB: What on earth is a CD, Mr. Murray?
>
> GM: Me nuh know what they have inna England, but out here a CD is a Certificate of Deposit. It mean say you get interest. So me do it.
>
> YB: Anything you say, Mr. Murray…

Gladstone Murray fostered the thirst for knowledge in so many young people who passed through The Barn over the years, not the least of whom was George Sinclair, for whom he was something of a father figure – for Mr. Murray, George was definitely a son. When Georgie died so young, so suddenly, so far away from home, it was a turning point, a moment from which I don't think Mr. Murray ever fully recovered.

Mr. Murray was not an easy man to get along with especially if you couldn't make up your mind, if your standards fell beneath what he considered to be correct, if you tried to get a Pepsi or a coconut water at the bar without paying for it – but he was always a man of principle, and man whom one could trust implicitly and A Jamaican Man For All Seasons.

Thank you Mr. Murray for all your care and attention over the years. May your good soul Rest in Peace.

George Silvera was one of Miss Girlie's sons. The large family lived at the rear of one of the houses in Norwood Avenue, one minute from The Barn. Miss Girlie used to wash the costumes for us, while Betty from the top office kept the auditorium clean. George was about five years of age when he made The Barn his second home. So did his younger brother, Charlie, and his sisters Rosie and Beverley, who all played their part in keeping the place a lively venue. Eventually George knew everything there was to know about the technical aspect of the place. He learned how to build sets, rig lighting, place speakers, re-solignum the walls. Everything. But he wasn't going to school. Trevor was instrumental in getting him into St. Andrew Technical School where he, Trevor, taught part time.

Georgie, as he was known to Munair, Trevor and I, but George to all others (this is a precise distinction), became a most reliable and popular technical director of theatre shows touring abroad from Jamaica. It was on one of these that he died of a heart ailment. An untimely death at too young an age, on the 27th November 2004. His allegiance to The Barn never faltered; no matter how grand his other commitments were, he was always there when The Barn needed him.

I have not attempted to squeeze the contribution of theatre people who were valued parts of the success of the place into the straightjacket of strictly consecutive comment. Nevertheless, in looking at the work presented during the twelve years, 1979-1992, a new pattern emerges. The original workers in the vineyard had by then dispersed and were ploughing individual theatrical, televisual, cinematic careers both at home in Jamaica and abroad.

It wasn't until the advent of Trevor Nairne, who brilliantly took over the role of artistic arbiter for a number of years, that some continuing artistic policy really began to emerge. This will be discussed in the chapter which follows.

CHAPTER NINE: TREVOR NAIRNE AT THE BARN, 1979-1992

Trevor Nairne: "The greatest explosion of new writing in the history of Jamaican theatre was concentrated in The Barn Theatre."

No theatrical enterprise can function to its maximum capacity and creativity without out a sensitive guiding light. In the first decade (1966 to 1977) of The Barn Theatre, the three foundations members jointly, and sometimes singly, performed this role with a commendable spirit of adventure, enlivened by many a turbulent moment in which the company numbers swung from the relatively large figure of seven equal partners to the rump of three and then to the rule of one.

When this period came to its natural end, as if on cue, there appeared on the horizon another Trevor. Nairne to be exact – a quietly spoken theatre person with a vision of the future theatre could have, should have, in Jamaica.

Trevor Nairne, O.D., has been described by Jamaican playwright and 2004 Musgrave medallist, Basil Dawkins, as a director's director... So begins the citation on the awarding of a Silver Musgrave Medal to Trevor Nairne for his contribution to Jamaican theatre.

In a short interview with him, conducted some time ago, he elaborated on the significance of The Barn theatre to Jamaica.

TN: Major trends in Jamaican theatre were influenced by the existence of The Barn Theatre. Chief among these was the provision of the facility for the exposition of Jamaican plays with a strong bias on work written by playwrights new to the business.

YB: When, in your opinion as a practising man of theatre, was the heyday of The Barn?[1]

TN: In the 80s and 90s, there was an establishment of a core of writers whose work was shown at The Barn and who have now come to dominate what I call commercial Jamaican theatre. These include Basil Dawkins, Patrick Brown, Aston Cooke, David Heron. Other important writers such as Alwin Bully, Hugh King, Stafford Ashani also first tried and tested out their skills there during that time.

The Barn continued to provide a platform for an extended number of writers well into the beginning of the 21st century, but it was plays like *Night Work* (Hugh King, 1978), *Killer* (Hugh King, 1980), *Undercover Lover* (Hugh King, 1988), *Cornflakes* (Patrick Brown, 1982), *Greasy Spoon* (Hugh King, 1982), *Ram Rod* (Hugh King, 1986), *Friends* (Patrick Brown, 1987), *Guava Jelly* (Patrick Brown, 1989), *Yard* (*Patrick Brown*, 1990), *December* (Patrick Brown, 1991), *Puppy Love* (Patrick Brown, 1996), and so on, which celebrated this new canon of Jamaican writing for the stage.

YB: Other trends?

TN: The introduction and implementation of the playwright producer or producer playwright was put into active practice at The Barn. This was a very significant influence on the future of theatre as it is now commercially practised here. The producer playwright is one of the most enduring facets of theatre in Jamaican theatre and this is where it was first introduced in any real way, with any real access to ordinary people. Playwrights quickly saw the advantages in having control over their product, over its revenue, the artistic elements; they saw the opportunities of making their work 'viable' in the market place. After all, Rhone had led the way with *Two Can Play*, which was a shining example of making the numbers work for the playwright. If two can pay why not have two in the play? Basil Dawkins in his two-hander *Champagne and Sky Juice* was obviously greatly influenced by Rhone's *Two Can Play*.

YB: Do you think the cult of the writer/producer format is the ultimate way of getting the best drama written and presented? Is this inevitable? Is there not a great temptation for the writer to curtail his/her imagination to the conditions of the takings at the box office and as a result possible great epics of Jamaican theatre have not been exposed or produced because the writer is also the producer with a weather eye on box office takings?

TN: I am in love with the Don Drummond story. Kwame Dawes has written it[2] and I want to direct it. I have put in an application to the Chase Foundation, but don't hold out much hope. It is of epic proportions and there is so much call on the slender resources Chase has at its disposal. Stafford Ashani has written "Killa Sound", which is also an epic, a magnificent sort of treatment of the psychology and history of music in Jamaica from the vintage to the cultural to the dance hall bling. It must be done. But who will? In a situation where there is so little experimentation in theatre in Jamaica, this would light up the sky, but it requires great imagination and lots of money to make it happen...

YB: Is there a case for public or large private subsidy?

TN: In the meantime the writer producer will prevail.

YB: Were there other developments encouraged by the existence of The Barn?

TN: We should look at the directors who emerged. Nearly all the now established directors working in Jamaica have worked at The Barn: Lloyd Reckord, Munair Zacca, Trevor Rhone, Alwyn Bully, Keith Noel, Eugene Williams, and of course you.

YB: And don't forget yourself, Trevor. Not many women. This persists...

TN: True.

YB: OK. Who are the Jamaican theatre directors of note who never worked at The Barn?

TN: I don't think Norman Rae ever did. Nor did Wycliffe Bennett. Stylistic incompatibility perhaps?

Trevor Nairne's first production at The Barn was the classic, almost flawless Derek Walcott play, *Remembrance*. Guyanese Eugene Williams, until recently director of the Jamaica School of Drama at the Edna Manley School of the Arts, was a member of the cast, as was Hugh Martin, Natalie Thompson and Brian Heap, among others.

I am grateful to Eugene Williams for his honest, detailed notes on this early production of such an important Caribbean play as *Remembrance*:

I came to Jamaica in September 1978 to study at the School of Drama and was probably recommended to Director Nairne by Dennis Scott or Lloyd Reckord, since I already had considerable experience as an actor in Guyana. Nevertheless, I recall being apprehensive about joining the cast who had already been rehearsing for several weeks. I was also in my first year of study and had already been coerced by Lloyd Reckord into the cast of his production of *Trial of The Cantonsville Nine*, at the school, the previous semester. As a first year student, I did not consider myself ready for exposure to the Jamaican audience. However Nairne, a recent graduate of the school, appeared to have been desperately in need of a replacement for the role of the young Interviewer in the mounting stages of the production.

I joined the cast at The Barn Theatre where I discovered that the producer of the production, Trevor Rhone, was apparently dissatisfied with aspects of his director's interpretation and/or casting and was noticeably anxious about his investment. Needless to say, this added to my anxiety in preparing for my first role on the professional Jamaican stage. Although I had never asked the question, I often wondered whether Rhone had fired my predecessor. I was therefore very eagerly awaiting notes from him in the rehearsals that he attended. I recall him intervening in a couple of rehearsals with the other actors, but he never treated any of my moments or offered any commentary, except once to correct my Guyanese creole pronunciation of "character". This was rather strange to me since the rest of the cast were not attempting to speak with Trinidadian accents, and the young interviewer could have been a Guyanese immigrant or a Trinidadian who did not venerate the Queen's English, as Walcott or Jordan did. But I conceded respectfully.

This tribute to the memory and passionate dedication of unsung heroes of foundational colonial sacrifices and education, set at a crucial political juncture of postcolonial resistance and commercial American intervention in the Caribbean, is crafted by Walcott with poignant resonances of history and moment, as well as creating compellingly recognisable characters.

However, I do not recall the production as a satisfying experience for me, and presumably for others, given its rather short run and limited audiences. My memory does not allow for a fair critique of the production from this distance, but I do recall the absence of the necessary tumult of anguished rage over colonial appropriations that Walcott and his surrogate protagonist embodies.

The role of Jordan is a monumental centre pole, which in our production hardly ever reached the necessary dramatic crescendos and elegance of poetic articulation of the text. Perhaps my dissatisfaction was also because I saw my role of the interviewer, then, as a mere dramatic device that facilitates Jordan's reminiscences and triggers the expressionistic recreation of history, memory and contemporary event. There is also an obvious generational theme, which, on later reflection, has given the experience more significance for me.

Remembrance was only the second Caribbean play (as opposed to Jamaican) to be presented at The Barn (Munair Zacca had directed *Sweet Talk* by Guyanese playwright Michael Abbensetts in 1977). While Walcott's *Remembrance* confined itself to the images, implications and cultural invasions of independence, Abbensetts *Sweet Talk*, wholly set in a cold-water flat in London, was concerned with the loss of financial independence and stultifying lack of creative opportunity that the talented Caribbean migrant to England suffered.

It was to be seven years before Trevor Nairne once again directed at The Barn although he was very much in control of the engine room during that period.

Trevor Nairne, always a serious and meticulous student of world theatre, brought to the programming of The Barn an eclectic imagination which is only rarely found in Jamaica's theatre circles these days. When, almost as a Damoclean sword, without his bidding, the artistic policy of the theatre fell on his shoulders, he brought quiet grace and charm to this onerous responsibility that had been thrust upon him.

During this time, new voices, faces and names – many of whom were to become essential to the development of The Barn aesthetic – were being seen and heard.

Trevor Nairne, whenever possible, flew the flag of "quality", taking on sensitive issue-based plays, for instance, David Heron's[3] *Against His Will,* addressing male sexual harassment. Nairne programmed this play, finding therein some variety from what was becoming the norm. The subject of this play was immediate and relevant; Heron was an exciting new writer with a refreshing, different approach. This production generated much discussion around a subject which was, and still is, very taboo in a Jamaican society, which tends towards the homophobic. Theatre should encourage thought and discussion. Should.

Among these new voices was that of Hugh King,[4] seven of whose plays were produced at The Barn over a period of ten years (1977-1988). At this time, Hugh King was a very familiar name in Jamaica, one might even use the word "celebrity", who attracted a lot of attention, especially as a radio personality. His first play at The Barn, *The Resurrection of Jonathan Digby*, was produced late in November 1977, followed by *Night Work* in 1979.

In 1980, his *Killer*, directed by Charmaine Creighton and boasting a stellar cast, was produced at The Barn. This was to be the beginning of a fruitful relationship in which he presented no fewer than seven of his works at the theatre. An interesting statistic suggests that a new Hugh King play always followed closely on the heels of a new Basil Dawkins work. *Flat Mate* preceded *Killer*; *Parson and Mrs. Jones* preceded *Greasy Spoon*; *Couples* preceded *Starting Over*; and finally *Couples* preceded *Ramrod* in 1986.

Hugh King was someone I had never actually met, but was anxious to. When I was back in Jamaica and looking for him, he was nowhere to be found. Some said, his "elevator no longer serviced the top floor" and so on. Having had much crueller comments made about me, this did not deter me, but truly, the search for Hugh King was intense, lasting for what seemed like an eternity, yet it remained stubbornly unfruitful. It was, however, important to find him, given the number of resounding successes he'd had at The Barn. Many theatre-goers remembered the plays, but sighed, *We have lost him*, or whispered, *He's gone to the hills*. Nevertheless, established, thoughtful theatre people, such as Basil Dawkins and Trevor Nairne, often referred to Hugh King and the impact his plays had made.

I finally found him in February 2015 through the quick wittedness of Scarlette Beharrie. He was, indeed, living in the hills. Kindly, he invited me to travel to St. Catherine in order to interview him. He would meet me somewhere along the road. OK.

During my first telephone conversation with him, he mentioned that he had for many years lived the life of a solitary Trappist monk. Secluded in the hills, he had taken vows of chastity and poverty, which he had maintained for well over two decades. He had existed without the usual modern conveniences – electricity and running water – only eating food

which he had produced personally. A photograph my research had un-
earthed showed him with flowing Rastafarian locks and advised of his
adopted name of Prince Nathanael.

Visiting him on the mountain became something exciting to look forward
to. However, minutes before setting off for the journey to the hills of St.
Catherine, a phone call from Hugh suggested that I might want to save myself
a difficult journey by meeting him in Kingston, at the Theatre Place[5]. I had
understood that he rarely visited the capital, not wanting to venture into
society, not wanting to leave his mystical mountain. I was a little puzzled at
this development but, fascinated, agreed to the change of venue.

Later in the day, when I drove into the Theatre Place car park for our
meeting, I saw a distinguished man of late middle age, sporting a trim grey
beard, dressed casually in American-type sportswear, talking in earnest to
a young man under a tree. I sat in the car to await the arrival of Hugh King/
Prince Nathanael. At the appointed time, I came out of the stifling car,
thinking to wait in the theatre where it might have been cooler. At that
moment, around turned the older man and it was he: Hugh King. No locks,
no robes, no attitude, just a big welcoming smile.

Some quick computing later, we were greeting each other.

During the short interview that followed, I learned that after attending
Old Harbour Primary School, he attended Beckford and Smith (St. Jago
High School) as had Trevor Rhone whom he called "cuz". He had studied
at Moore Business school, after which he went to the New York School of
Announcing and Speech, in the footsteps of the cult radio announcer, "El
Numero Uno", Don Topping.

Returning home to Jamaica, he soon became quite the man about town,
working at Graphic Arts, successfully selling life insurance exclusively to
women, of course. Basil Dawkins remembers him once conducting an on-
air competition to guess the price of the red silk shirt he was wearing. The
prize was dinner with himself, the main man, the Captain, as he liked to be
called. He was a well-known debonair character around town, a radio
announcer with an avid following, who lived in expensive Beverley Hills
overlooking Kingston, drove a BMW, and always exhibited an extreme
fondness for female company of the more exotic variety.

Eventually in 1977, he turned his hand to playwriting. I asked him what
had brought him to such a solitary discipline.

Hugh King told me:

From an early age I used to dress up in my grandmother's large dresses
and perform comedy sketches for my delighted grandparents. My

grandfather accompanied by playing his accordion. I studied English Literature at St. Jago and learned life lessons from Shakespeare, especially *Twelfth Night* and *The Merchant of Venice*. The first play I ever saw performed was my first play, *The Resurrection of Jonathan Digby*. I had never seen a play before!

It turned out that he was one of the group of playwrights who found a refuge in The Barn. He said:

I was a newcomer. I knew nothing about play production so I thought I had to do everything myself: write, act, direct, design: everything. I knew no one, but Carmen Tipling encouraged Mr. Murray to give me a break and George helped too. That's how my first play, *The Resurrection of Jonathan Digby*, saw the light of the stage in 1977. The Barn was an embryonic encasement for me.

Hugh King went on to become one of the hottest playwrights at The Barn for a decade, with sensational hits, and even international success on Britain's Channel 4 television network where his *Body Moves*,[5] which started life at The Barn in 1984, was televised in Britain as a sitcom, to great acclaim.

Fellow playwright Basil Dawkins readily praises *Night Work* as does critic and academic Mervyn Morris who knows a thing or two about Jamaican theatre as he, it is said , has missed very few plays which have been produced in Jamaica over many decades. Other memorable King scripts include *Greasy Spoon* 1982, *Starting Over* 1985, *Ramrod* 1986 and the explosive and fondly remembered *Undercover Lover* which brought his playwriting career to an abrupt end, despite its overwhelming box office success.

So what did Hugh King write about?

The answer is simple; the triumph of good over evil. Each of my plays deals with challenging social situations involving decaying family values, prostitution, drugs, illiteracy, sexual insufficiency, and so on.

As a result of the successful translation of his play *Body Moves* into a televised situation comedy in Great Britain, Hugh went to London and struck up a good working relationship with Gloria Hamilton and her theatre company, Umoja. It was during this time that he attended London University, where he studied Sociology and was awarded both a Bachelors and a Masters Degree. It was when he was about to undertake his Doctorate of Philosophy that his life took another direction. He found God. And his playwriting ceased.

In 2015, however, having navigated an almost complete circle, Hugh King's seminal *Night Work* was being rehearsed for presentation in Kingston at The Theatre Place,[6] directed by its original 1978 director, Pablo Hoilett, with Hugh King himself in the lead. Unfortunately, this production suffered from lack of proper marketing. Hugh admits the changing times and necessities of theatre had surprised him, he who had last ventured into production when times were slower and kinder.

What had finally brought Hugh King down from the hills and back into Babylon? He did not say at first, but recently explained to me that the spirit had returned him to the place from whence he had been taken decades before. The circle, it appears, is complete.

Endnotes

1. Nairne was still at school in 1965 when The Barn was first thought of. As there was no written record (until now) of the theatre's early pioneering work in the 60s and 70s, it is not surprising that younger member of the Jamaican theatre community have no reference point beyond their own experience. (YB)
2. This play will appear in 2018 in *Kwame Dawes: Four Plays* (Peepal Tree Press).
3. David Heron, playwright, producer and actor. His plays include, *The Infidel* (1985), *Ecstasy* (1994), *Intermission* (1996), *Against His Will* (1998), *Love and Marriage and New York City* (1999), *Redemption* (2003) and *4Play* (2005). His plays have attracted success in Jamaica, North America and the UK. See *The Jamaican Theatre: Highlights...*, pp 282-282.
4. See "King Returns with *Night Work*", *The Gleaner*, 1 May, 2015.
5. *Body Moves* was a UK TV film directed by Lloyd Reckord in 1987.
6. Theatre Place: one of the newer better equipped middle scale sized theatres in Kingston managed by veteran theatre director and producer Pablo Hoilett who cut his theatrical teeth at The Barn. Unfortunately it has now closed its doors.

CHAPTER TEN: THE WOMEN

Women have not featured regularly in the driving seat of Jamaica's theatre industry, as directors, designers, playwrights or producers. Female actors abound. Greta Fowler was a powerful theatre producer in the mid 20th century, and in the 21st century Barbara Gloudon is without doubt a powerful member of the Little Theatre Movement, for which she appears to write all the annual pantomime scripts. Recent forays into the area of playwriting and directing by female actor Dahlia Harris[1] have been successful and are to be welcomed.

This situation was not much different decades ago at The Barn, although there were some remarkable challengers to the status quo.

There was Kay Osbourne, all rounder, winner in 1967 of the Miss Jamaica Nation Beauty Contest, keen cricketer, who was to become General Manager of the Jamaica Broadcasting Corporation, turned successful playwright in 1978 with *Wipe That Smile*. When asked about her memories of The Barn and the influence it had on her literary career she said:

> The Barn Theatre was a small and unique performance space where the majority black population's voice took centre stage during a brief period of fervent social and political public conversation that included theatre people. This theatre was a godsend for the period's storytelling as it provided an important space in which actors performed multidimensional roles that neither required elaborate sets nor tortuous costumes, which would have been out of place there.
>
> At The Barn, fearless and talented writers revealed yet unspoken truths about life in Jamaica and elsewhere that challenged the status quo, while providing gut-busting entertainment. The tight space facilitated textured emotional exchanges between audiences and performers who played off the audience's single-minded focus that often included shouted instructions on what actors should do next. Compelling stories and extraordinary performances occurred nightly, resulting in word-of-mouth campaigns that lured throngs of loyal Barn-theatre-goers, night after night.
>
> This intense environment prompted my interest in writing *Wipe That Smile*, which explored the travails and ultimate redemption of Phanso, the ghetto sufferer who was at a crossroad in his life; Putus, the religious fanatic who blamed devil's disciple, Prettywalks, for leading her man

Phanso astray; Prettywalks who spoke glib truths and attracted trouble; Rasta elder, Dread, who "bun dung Babylon" to save his son; Miss Scarlett, the cheating browning bitch, and the ever-present yet unseen big man, Mr. Palmer.

The story idea was born inside The Barn Theatre. While watching a performance, it occurred to me that I could write such a story. Upon completion, Trevor Rhone read the script, liked it, and encouraged me to get it produced. I decided to produce it myself. The rest is history.

In many ways, *Wipe That Smile* broke new ground as it put on display realities of life as a sufferer in Jamaica that remained unexplored until then. During performances, audiences laughed out loud and wept in despair; it was among the first Jamaican plays to enjoy full-to-capacity houses for each performance during a subsequent tour of the island and for every performance in Canada, the UK and the USA, including off-off Broadway, where audiences responded with unrestrained enthusiasm.

Without a doubt, *Wipe That Smile* is as relevant today as it was when it was written and first produced in the 1970s.

It is important not to lose sight of the fact that during the forty years of The Barn's existence, Carmen Tipling, whose work has been discussed earlier, was the first woman to have a play produced when, in 1974, her *Straight Man* was presented. She repeated this achievement in 1976 with the presentation of her second play, *Skeleton Inside*. In 1978 Kay Osbourne was only the second woman to have her play, *Wipe That Smile*, produced in this theatre. Things changed fundamentally on this front with the magical appearance of the Sistren Theatre Collective.

The long association between Sistren and The Barn begun with the presentation of their very first play, *Bellywoman Bangarang* in 1978, directed by Honor Ford Smith.[2]

At first it was only a five-minutes-long improvisation encouraged by Honor Ford Smith. The actors were women on the Government Impact Programme – or what was better known then as the "Crash Programme", in which women thought unskilled were employed by the Government to clean the streets. Many of these women were moved from the Crash Programme, sweeping streets, into becoming teaching assistants who looked after the welfare of children in grades 5 and 6 in schools. This was part of the solution to the confusion caused by the shift system that operated in schools at the time. Known as "hot seating", everyday, there were sometimes three completely different sets of students using the facilities of the school. It was an admirable third-world solution to overcome the excesses of an ever-growing population, but an administrative and logistic nightmare. Out of the

many women who were thus employed, a small group, with the encouragement of the late Dr. Olive Lewin (1927-2013), musicologist, social anthro-
pologist and founder of the Jamaica Folk singers, were persuaded to perform
a short skit at the workers' day concert at the all-age school where they were
employed. After much misgiving, they mimed the skit, which was very well
received by the audience. It was these women who became the Sistren
Theatre Collective, and a significant relationship between The Barn and the
vibrant Sistren Theatre Company began at this juncture.

Bellywoman Bangarang[3], nurtured and directed by Honor Ford Smith,
dealt with the issues of teenage pregnancy, mother and daughter relationships and relationships between men and women. This was Sistren's first
full-blown production, followed in 1979 by *Bandoolu Version*.

Honor Ford Smith writes:

Sistren first performed *Bellywoman Bangarang* at The Barn in 1978 (directed
by me). That was a wonderful occasion – it was based on improv, so
you never knew when it was going to end. It was hailed as a breakthrough
in Jamaican theatre. That was because it was a response to the social
movement of the time of independence when women were simultaneously
required to be strong and invulnerable at the same time as they were
domesticated. It was a collective creation based on the life stories of
the women of Sistren as performed by them. Opening night was followed
by an earthquake and my grannie dying. Your family officiated at both
the *Bellywoman* and the death and burial of my granny (also theatrical...
as dying is always a *tour de force*). *Bellywoman* was made possible at The
Barn because YOU – and was it Trevor Nairne then? – allowed us the
theatre at a reduced rate. In 1979, we did *Bandoolu Version* (also directed
by me). That one opened at the Bellevue Garden Theatre, which was
later destroyed, and then later moved uptown to The Barn. In 1981,
Sistren's *QPH* opened [named after the leading characters, Queenie,
Pearlie, Hopie]. It was based on the lives of the women who died in a
fire that consumed the old colonial almshouse where they were housed.
The fire happened during the fighting leading up to the 1980 election
and it dramatised the ways in which the bodies of impoverished black
women got treated as disposable. *QPH* was the favourite of all Sistren's
plays, brilliantly directed by Hertencer Lindsay, and it played to excellent
houses. Coming into being just after Independence, The Barn performed
exactly what was needed and is still needed – a space for innovation,
love, economy and commitment.

The company was awarded an OAS (Organisation of American States)
grant to allow it to perform *Bandoolu Version* in the community. A member
of the cast, Bev Didi Eliot, lived near Bellevue Hospital, so was able to

involve her community in East Kingston in support of the play. It was also an opportunity to support the downtown Garden Theatre, which Bellevue's leading psychiatrist, Freddie Hickling, had founded at the hospital as part of an attempt to explore, theatrically, the idea of healing people from the ills of colonialism, principally from the way in which colonial power had deemed and made black folks' resistance pathological. Bellevue is Jamaica's principal centre for the treatment of mental illness.

Hilary Nicholson, a close colleague of Honor Ford Smith, also worked untiringly for the Collective. She recalled:

> I was very involved with Sistren's *Bellywoman Bangarang*. I did PR and overall coordination work. It was HARD work; working with Sistren was always hard work,
>
> I was amazed by Honor's extraordinary creative and innovative directing! I remember audience reactions were VERY mixed; some were shocked, others confused at some of the symbolism we used, some loved it. We (Honor, Sistren, me and Ja society) were all new to the idea of mounting a play like that in Jamaica! It was very personal, coming from the members' own lives, the abuse and sexual violence they experienced.
>
> I think it was during *B/Bangarang* that one actress's babyfather came there to attack her, and threatened to mash up the place and we had to whisk her away to safety and get the police onto him... She was "neglecting" her family duties by being out at night...
>
> I was fully involved in many different ways with Sistren, coordinating, road manager, lighting person, pr, financial coordinator, general resource person...

In 1987, Sistren's *Buss Out* was written by playwright and artistic director, Pat Cumper. Nearly thirty years on she looks back:

> Over the years, I went to The Barn Theatre to see a range of work, and it was a major part of Kingston's theatre offering, particularly for the production of new Caribbean writing. There, I saw other new plays by Trevor Rhone and others. And after going to university and then beginning to build a career as a playwright myself, I saw my own work on that tiny stage. Earl Warner had been asked to work with the ground-breaking theatre company, Sistren, to create a show around housing, and particularly the behaviour of ghetto landlords with their female tenants. By this time, Sistren was very skilled at working with improvisation and Earl directed these improvisations, while I observed and then was sent away to write *Buss Out*. My draft was knocked into shape and then eventually produced, to good reviews, at The Barn. I remember the leading actress coming off stage, with the enthusiastic applause of the audience ringing in her ears, and giving me a huge hug for my work on the play. In my usual inhibited way, I had no idea how to respond, which made her laugh,

but the image of being with the cast celebrating outside the dressing rooms, as the audience left the theatre, has always stayed with me.

The final Sistren production to be hosted at The Barn was *Mirro Mirro* in 1997. This production was a more formal development in the way the company worked.

Jean Small,[4] distinguished theatre practitioner and academic, who directed the Sistren Collective in *Nana Ya* and *Mirro Mirro* wrote:

Working with the Sistren Theatre Collective was a new, creative and sometimes daunting experience for me, as it would have been for anyone coming out of mainstream theatre and having to do theatre with a grassroots group. Up to the time, when I was invited to direct a play with them in 1994, they were still a largely illiterate group of women, but like most Jamaican people, they were very culturally aware of themselves as Jamaicans, well versed in the Jamaican language, songs, proverbs and values of the environment from which they originated. They, therefore, had the physical and verbal tools for dramatic expression.

As they were known by that time as a group of women who explored issues concerning women, I was invited to develop a dramatic production with them on Nanny, the Jamaican heroine [leader of the Maroons in the 18th Century]. Jamaicans are so proud of their national heroes that one would think that this would be an easily manageable topic. However, this Collective was already known for what is called "Oral Theatre". They would be given a topic, which they would develop and play out in their inimitable style. It was not so easy working on the subject of Nanny, because I discovered they knew nothing of their history. They knew nothing about slavery. The word "Ashanti" had no significance for them. Up to this time, Sistren had been creating plays that got their cultural context from their own lives. This was the first time that they were going to create a dramatic production on a topic outside of their personal lives. They needed first to be educated.

The dramatic work went into pause as we visited the library, looked at pictures and learnt about displacement, loss of name, religion and language. It was not until they had some understanding of the historical experience that I could demand of them some imaginative dramatic creation of one of the themes. As they could not read or write, the process was entirely oral, that is they spoke and I recorded all that they said. That material I refined into a final script, but they owned the songs and their own colourful Jamaican language. *Nana Yah*, as the play was called, conveyed the meaning that the spirit of Nanny lives on in the women of today. This was very empowering to the actresses. The play was performed on the lawns behind the Devon Great House, which was an innovative use of space.

By 1997, when we embarked on *Mirro Mirro*, there had been some significant changes in the personnel of the company. Some of the older

members had left and younger members had joined the Collective. They
were more educated and brought a different energy to the work. They
wanted to discuss sexuality in this production and as we started out without
a script, it was an opportunity for us to work at making a script from
scratch, without knowing exactly in which direction it would go. We
began by talking about their sexuality and reducing the discussions to
individual words, which formed the core of the production. The content
was again turned back on their own lives and as director I had to respect
their interpretations of the words, which were closely related to their
own life experiences.

Some of their interpretations were culturally unfamiliar to me, but
they were valid to them and to a Jamaican audience. In some cases, it
was an exposure of practices and behaviour that they had never spoken
about publicly, and this was very emotionally cleansing for them. It had
the same effect on members of the audience. On one night of the
performance, a gentleman and his female companion, looking for some
evening's entertainment, decided to sit in on the production. At the end
of the production, the gentleman said it was too emotionally demanding
to be considered entertainment.

The nature of Sistren's work took a hard look at the reality of women's
lives and it must have been at about this period that the theatre fare in
Jamaica changed more to comedy. *Mirro Mirro* was the last major production that the Sistren Theatre Collective did.

In Jamaican society then, except for the Pantomime at the Ward Theatre,
and fondly remembered Sunday morning cabaret shows, it could be said
that theatre was considered a light pursuit for the educated, better-off
members of the middle and upper classes. The emergence of Sistren
Theatre Collective was perhaps the greatest social watershed in the history
of Jamaican theatre. Those involved with contemporary Jamaican theatre
should salute them.

Among the women who made their mark on the work of The Barn was
Grace McGhie (now Brown). The next chapter celebrates her contribution
to this theatre's work.

Endnotes

1. See the *Jamaica Observer*, "Some things you (probably) never knew
    about…Dahlia Harris" (22 March 2014). At the time of the interview,
    she had written 24 plays and produced 7. Her best known plays
    include *Thicker Than Water, Judgement, God's Way* and most recently,
    Country Wedding (2017).
2. Honor Ford Smith (1951-) studied theatre at the University of

Wisconsin-Madison. She edited and contributed to Sistren's book *Lionheart Gal* (1986). She edited *3 Jamaican Plays: A Postcolonial Anthology* (2011). Her own collection of poems, *My Mother's Last Dance* was published in 1996.

3. *Bellywoman Bangarang* was published by University of The Virgin Islands.

4. Jean Small is a Guyanese-Jamaican since 1954. Her plays include *A Black Woman's Tale*, and she developed a one-woman show, "The Awful Truth" (2015). She is director of TALA (Theatre Arts Learning Aids) and taught at UWI Mona. See www.theatreartsja.com/about-jean-small and *The Gleaner*, 5 April, 2015.

CHAPTER ELEVEN: GRACING THE BARN

As has been noted already, during the forty year existence of The Barn, relatively few plays by women were presented on that small stage. In 1968 one of the co-authors of *It's Not My Fault Baby*, Jackson Martin, eventually turned out to be the pseudonym of Sonia Mills. Some six years later, Carmen Tipling, fresh from working in the script department at Warner Brothers in the USA, produced her *Straight Man*. *The Skeleton Inside* followed in 1976. As noted earlier, Kay Osbourne produced her *Wipe That Smile* in 1978.

Thereafter, as outlined in the previous chapter, Sistren Collective was an imposing presence. After Sistren's demise, a compilation of work, *Hot Flashes*, culled from writers as diverse Jamaica Kincaid, Barbara Raskin, Miriama Ba, Jean Rhys and Lillian Rubin, was staged in 1996, and in 2002, Marcia L. Leslie's *The Trial of One Short-Sighted Black Woman* (1999),[1] produced by the National Theatre Trust, was followed by Andrea Daley Salmon's *Death Row* in the same year.

When one considers that upwards of one hundred and fifteen plays by men were presented at The Barn during the forty years of its existence, the dozen or so female outings are disappointingly low, signalling that very little progress has been made in this area in Jamaican theatre.

When the representation of women directors is analysed, the story is even worse. If one ignores the first years, when, as one of the founding members of the theatre I directed some ten productions – eight before leaving for the UK in 1971, and *School's Out* in 1974 and *Bellas Gate Boy* in 2002 – the record is quite appalling. In 1971, Eileen Porter directed *What the Butler Saw*. In 1973, Melba Bennett did a reworking of *Comic Strip*. Honor Ford Smith, Hertencer Lindsay and Jean Small directed between them four of the five Sistren plays – only six directorial credits, with Honor Ford Smith receiving two of these.

The record is thankfully better where the roll call of female actors is concerned. The stage has been graced repeatedly by so many female actors, women of distinction such as Leonie Forbes, Barbara McCalla Lee, Claudia Robinson, Pauline Cowan Kerr, Ruth Ho Shing, Fae Ellington, Christine Bell... The list is endless and impressive.

However, amongst them all, there reigned supreme Grace McGhie Brown, the first lady of The Barn. Her presence on The Barn stage, gives her a position of enduring authority. I never had the good fortune to work with her – something I have always regretted – but I have nevertheless always thought of her as our first lady. Her versatility, her centred space, her generosity on stage… When I approached her with a few questions, her reaction to this title was just what one might have imagined from this brilliant, understated actor: gracious. She kindly answered some questions which offer a close-up view and appreciation of what it was like to be so often part and parcel of The Barn.

YB: Tell me about your association with The Barn.
GB: My association with The Barn began in October 1971 with *Smile Orange* [remember the receptionist?] by Trevor Rhone, directed by Dennis Scott and starred Carl Bradshaw, Stan Irons, Vaughn Crosskill, Beth Hyde, and Glen Morrison as Buss Boy. In early 1973, *Sala*, written by Slade Hopkinson, also directed by Dennis Scott – with Teddy Price as Little Roy, and a really great actor – David ? – from Anguilla who was a student at UWI at the time – can't remember his last name – he was my husband… Anyway Christine Bell was Sala. Fae Ellington took over that role for a short period [with 2 days' notice] while Christine went off to have an emergency appendectomy! Later in 1973 there was *Comic Strip*, written by Trevor and again directed by Scott. He really paid a major role in carving out my formative years in theatre – he [and Trevor] practically taught me all I know. The cast also included Roy Case and Bobb Kerr [alternating] as my "white man" lover with Carl Bradshaw as my Jamaican man; then *Sleeper* in 1973 by Trevor and directed by Dennis.
   Fast forwarding to the nineteen-nineties: in 1991, there was also another major production, which was directed by Pablo Hoilett and had Karl Binger as my husband [alternating with Trevor Fearon] and John Jones as the psychiatrist. The name of the play is *Deloris*. In 1992 there was *Bedtime Stories*, skits produced by Ed Wallace, directed by Bari Johnson, also starred Karl Binger and Pearl McFarlane. I was named Best Actress for this role, as well as for *Champagne & Sky Juice* in 1998.
   Hot Flashes was in 1995. It was actually produced by Alwin Bully, who was UNESCO's representative, and headed up the local International Theatre Institute at the time. The script was adapted and directed by Henk Tjon and the cast was: Leonie Forbes, Jean Small, Fae Ellington, Marjorie Whylie, Barbara McCalla, and Grace McGhie. The story was about six friends who had been apart for many years and had arranged to meet for a reunion. Each was at a crossroad in her life. The 7th friend "Sukie" had died, so was missing from the reunion. She was represented by her little shitzu dog, who played a very poignant role.

YB: I always think of you as the First Lady of The Barn. How do you react to that title?

GB: I'm a little uncomfortable with it. Feels a little presumptuous to me... After all, I would certainly reserve that title for you! Would really prefer if you omitted it, although I do like "Gracing The Barn"...

YB: My research shows that over a period of some twenty-seven years, from 1971 to 1998, you appeared on The Barn stage in no fewer than fourteen productions. Do you have any special memories of any of these plays/productions?

GB: Yes... the "box" to the cheek I received every night from Natalie Thompson, who played my mother in *Sleeper* – it was painfully real one night, when she left her handprint on my jaw! Playing topless [with back to audience] in a bedroom scene with Roy Case in *Comic Strip. A* wonderful dance sequence of two senior citizens with Karl Binger in *Bedtime Stories*, and taking instruction from Dr. Freddie Hickling, the psychiatrist, on how to play a psychotic in *Deloris*... Incidentally, I just remembered the name of the leading male actor in *Sala*, which I've been searching for... it's David Carty. He was a student from Anguilla, studying at UWI at the time... He was a terrifically talented young actor, who we hoped would stay in Jamaica after graduation, but he returned to Anguilla to teach and act... a real loss to Jamaican theatre! I remember he also did a two-hander called *Zoo Story* at Creative Arts. It was a mind-blowing performance... but I ramble...

YB: No problem at all. Over the years you were directed by some of Jamaica's most renowned directors: Dennis Scott four times, Trevor Rhone twice, Keith Noel twice, Charles Hyatt, Bari Johnson, Henk Tjon, Trevor Nairne, Pablo Hoilett and Buddy Pouyat... Would you share the single most memorable moment with any of these directors?

GB: Dennis Scott taught me theatre discipline, and how to trust my emotions in finding the character. You learnt very early never to arrive even five minutes late for any of his rehearsals. Henk Tjon taught us how to cement the lines before each performance – simply run the lines straight through at breakneck speed. It certainly worked!

YB: Experience/exposure to these nine different directors must have given you food for thought. They were all male (nothing strange in Jamaican theatre even now) and must have come from different perspectives. (e.g. Charles Hyatt from actor to director, Trevor directing his own work); do you remember any of their varying approaches to rehearsals, the analysis of the script, the freedom of the actor? Were any of them from the "push and pull" school of directing?

GB: It was very instructive watching Trevor "block" a scene. He never moved from a page of script until it was right. Many times he would abandon a rehearsal if something wasn't working, and go home to "fix" the script. When he returned with new inspiration next rehearsal, it was always right.

YB: OK. You worked with Carl Bradshaw in *Smile Orange*. He was very new to theatre, having just completed *The Harder They Come* straight from the Excelsior High School staff room. He was the sports master. How did he adapt?

GB: You know *Smile Orange* had a one-year run at The Barn, and followed up with extensive touring island wide, ending in 1973! Carl was a "natural" in the role of Ringo... His enthusiasm just had to be tempered at times! Unfortunately, he never stayed with the stage, but moved on to greener pastures in films.

YB: Are there any other actors you would like to mention?

GB: I learnt a lot from Charlie [Hyatt][2] – both as actor and director... His attention to detail, and his timing were legendary. He demanded excellence, especially from himself, at all times.

YB: Would you comment on the content of the plays, or some of the plays you acted in, including the depth of characterization and subtlety the playwrights exhibited? Maybe even the content of the plays in what was still nearly a newly Independent Jamaica.

GB: *Two Can Play* was very special. "Gloria" and "Jim" are two hard-working, honest Jamaicans who set out to achieve a better life for their family during seriously difficult times in Jamaica. They were willing to take real chances, despite the odds. We all know people like this – and Trevor was able to give us, the actors, full rein! A truly powerful script, and exciting to play. I miss Trevor, and Charlie.

YB: How do you see the future of theatre in Jamaica?

GB: I'm very hopeful... I see a growing crop of young, talented, actors, who are learning their craft. They need our support and encouragement, and certainly, they need the right scripts, directors, and producers. Because we must be careful not to get bogged down in mediocrity. Most of all, there is need for adequate theatre space. We have lost too many venues in Kingston lately. Perhaps it's part of our present economic struggle. It is going to take hands and hearts working together to achieve a continued healthy, vibrant theatre for our people, and not just in Kingston.

YB: And finally?

GB: I have actually had to spend many hours doing extensive research into my association with The Barn – trying to get it right – the times, dates, and details of writers, directors, producers, etc.... so that we have the record straight... Believe me, remembering details of 30 - 40 years ago have been quite challenging, so I had to seek help... but it was really enjoyable and stimulating to make contact with my friends in the theatre and relive some of the times we spent together!

YB: First lady you surely are. Thank you so much.

A note on Charles Hyatt: This is what I wrote on the occasion of his death:

> Some called him Charles but he will always be Charlie to me. We go back to the early seventies, when he was a well-known actor in London and kindly agreed to play Ringo in my production of *Smile Orange*, which toured London as a major part of Jamaica's 10th Anniversary Independence celebrations. His attention to detail, his instinctive understanding and compassion, his flawless timing were all indispensable elements of the success of the production which brought out homesick Jamaicans in their thousands. Despite the easy humour, the quick asides, the naughty winks, Charlie was at heart a quiet, serious thinker, who spent time studying in detail the social and racial history of our people and was a font of knowledge on old time Jamaica. I was powerfully reminded of this every time we met or worked together over the past thirty five years.
>
> So, my old friend walk good and keep them laughing wherever you are.

Yvonne Brewster, London Jan 3rd 2007

Endnotes

1. The full title adds *v Mammy Louise and Safreeta Mae* (New York: Broadway Play Publishing Inc. 2002).
2. Charles Hyatt, legendary Jamaican actor died at the age of 75 in the USA. See note at end of chapter. He wrote the charming memoir, *When Me Was A Boy* (UWI Press, 2007).

CHAPTER TWELVE: COLLABORATIONS, PARTNERSHIPS, NEW DIRECTIONS

The close confines of The Barn may have contributed to the number of meaningful collaborations that blossomed there.

Successful creative collaboration is not always simple. However, in the forty years' existence of The Barn Theatre there have been many instances where the difficulty of continuing creative collaboration did not deter progress, indeed proved inspiring, to wit the first few years. Starting in 1965, these were filled with personal dramas, but given what all thought was the overwhelming importance of the work, it was collaboration that always won the day… keeping a sense of focus on the main prize. Thought-provoking theatre.

There was, for instance, as noted earlier, the close working relationship between Barn founder member Munair Zacca and Stafford Ashani, which was intellectually challenging, theatrically rewarding and enterprising, resulting in brave new offerings such as *The Quickie*.

But collaboration between theatre artists is often fraught with lively dialogue and dissension, sometime verging on the physical. Louis Marriott, a Jamaican playwright and producer of distinction, in 1988 co-authored a musical revue *One Stop Driver* with Trevor Rhone. This exercise exhibited all the hallmarks of an unhappy collaboration, as disagreements between the co-authors/producers and the director/producer seemed to overwhelm the product. Resignations, press releases, and creative misunderstandings all contributed to a less than happy product.

As outlined in Chapter Nine, during the years 1977-1999, Trevor Nairne was in all but name the artistic director of The Barn. It was he who determined what went on. He kept in constant touch with me and we would meet on my annual visits to the island. I was impressed with the sophistication of his overview, his programming: imaginative, modern, farsighted and fit for purpose. Particularly important was his relationship with the playwright, Patrick Brown.

Patrick Brown's first play, *Cornflakes*, had been presented at The Barn in 1982. Directed by Keith Noel, it starred Clive "Uzu" Anderson, Rosemary

Murray, Hope Blake, Calvin Butler, Winston Tucker and Kenny Salmon. However, it was in 1987 when Nairne's close professional relationship with Patrick Brown started at The Barn, when he directed Brown's play, *Friends*. This was the beginning of a long and fruitful collaboration between these two important Jamaican theatre artists. Between 1987 and 1999 Trevor Nairne directed ten plays at The Barn, six of which were written by Patrick Brown, and they have continued to work as a dynamic team to the present time with such recent comedy successes as *Ladies of the Night*, *Breadfruit Kingdom* and in 2015, *Saving Alligator High*, which bears some similarity in theme to *School's Out*. Nairne and Brown form perhaps the longest collaboration of this kind in Jamaican theatre.

The 1987 production of *Friends* was followed in 1989 by *Guava Jelly*. 1989 and 1990 saw two versions of Yard… *Yard 89* and *Yard 90*. The lovely, moving *December* followed in 1991, and after a break of some five years *Puppy Love* was the final Patrick Brown play to be directed by Trevor Nairne at The Barn.

Nairne also directed two plays, *Ecstasy* (1994) and *Against His Will* (1999), by David Heron and also Stafford Ashani's *Foreign Mind* and *Run For Your Wife*, which was a Jamaican adaptation of an English comedy by Ray Cooney. This production saw the beginning of other long-lasting professional relationships, with Lennie Salmon and Glen Campbell, which bore fruit in the foundation of two professional producing companies: Better Theatre Productions and its very successful successor, Jam Biz, which is currently probably the most professional production company in the island.

There was also the Aston Cooke/Michael Nicholson team of writer and director, which had an impressive record at The Barn. Aston Cooke was one of the newcomers in 1998 who became one of the playwrights who produced much of their work at the theatre. His collaboration with director Michael Nicholson became an important feature of his work in no fewer than five productions he presented between 1998 and 2005. The titles of his plays might just suggest the subject matter: 1998, *Front Room;* 2000, *Country Duppy;* 2001, *Kiss Mi Neck;* 2003, *Single Entry,* and finally, in 2005, *Jamaica2Rahtid*, which brought the curtain down on The Barn stage forever. This revue-type entertainment was inoffensive and the audience enjoyed it, but to my mind it sadly lacked intellectual challenge.

For quite some time I had been aware of changing perceptions and audience expectations in Jamaica. Audiences arrived at the theatre expecting to see reflections of their lives on stage, coupled with the Jamaican talent for self-parody. They wanted to be presented with situations that required

quick thinking and not a small dollop of Anansi mentality to be solved. To
satisfy this demand was a pressing consideration for producers. The new
audiences also wanted to laugh. Loudly. At everything. There began a
tradition of failure at the box office if more serious plays, plays of literary
merit, were offered. The prevalence of revue-type entertainment was part
of this process. I was far from alone in regretting this development.

Theatre critic Michael Reckord, a member of the distinguished Jamaican theatre dynasty observed:

> Theatre in Jamaica was traditionally – before Independence – a reflection
> of the tastes of the elite. Contemporary theatre, now largely locally written,
> has become coarser, even vulgar – reflecting the tastes of the broader
> society, and rejecting colonial values. It now appeals to larger, more diverse
> audiences and, despite its flaws, is a source of pride to many. Because
> of its near-exclusive focus on formula comedy, it is less suitable as a
> learning tool for theatre students who need the nourishment of serious
> drama and creativity.
>
> Generally speaking, The Barn's productions exhibited the positive
> elements of the lists and avoided the negative ones, and comprised
> mainstream (as opposed to "roots"[1]) fare.

Often the external onlooker sees most of the game. Penny Smith[2], a
Trinidadian with close Jamaican associations, reflects on the possible
causes for the change of theatrical preference in Jamaica:

> Quality theatre no longer seems to appeal to the great majority of Jamaica's
> theatre-going public. There appears to be little appetite for the works
> of C.L.R. James, Derek Walcott, Wole Soyinka and the like, not to mention
> Shakespeare. What the bulk of Jamaicans who visit the theatre
> overwhelmingly support is "roots" theatre, a form of light, bawdy comedy
> many considered degenerate. These plays are filled with sexual innuendo
> and written completely in patois foreigners find difficult to understand.
>
> Why this change in the tastes of Jamaica's theatre-going public? Others
> have observed similar changes in cultural tastes right across the Caribbean.
> There are undoubtedly complex reasons for this. However, I feel a key
> reason is the migration from the island of sectors of the middle class.
>
> When Michael Manley swept into power in the early 1970s, he introduced
> a radical socialist agenda that favoured the poor and turned Jamaica upside
> down. In pursuit of his socialist dream, Manley cosied up to Fidel Castro
> and even welcomed Cuban specialists to the island to advise on workers'
> cooperatives and to build schools. Jamaica's well-educated middle classes
> became nervous. For them, this socialist dream was a nightmare. But
> Manley was resolute. If you don't like it, he declared, there are five flights
> a day to Miami. Many took his advice. They packed up and fled the

country in droves, taking their money as well as their more "high brow" cultural and artistic tastes with them. There is much talk about how Jamaica has been adversely affected by a "brain drain". Well, my feeling is that a "cultural drain" has also taken place, which has been equally impoverishing for the island.

Manley's flirtation with socialism came at a high price. Jamaica was left grappling with years of negative growth, high unemployment, spiralling inflation and frightening levels of violence. One can see how many would be desperate for light, comic relief (rather than more cerebral productions) in the face of the increasingly more difficult day-to-day struggles of putting food on the table and a roof over one's head.

The thing is, I suspect, that this mass migration of Jamaica's educated middle class also impoverished the lives of these migrants themselves. Jamaican friends speak of relatives who were regular patrons of the theatre and all things cultural in Jamaica. Yet after migrating to America, their lives became centred on work, home and shopping malls with "All You Can Eat" buffets. Some might fit church in, but there were few visits to museums, art galleries, theatres and the like. It is as if they switched into survival mode, as they grappled with underemployment and the much harsher living and working conditions typically faced by America's immigrant communities, leaving them little time, energy or money to indulge in the arts.

Sadly, it may well be that, artistically speaking, the mass migration of the Jamaican middle classes had few winners and many losers, all round.

Endnotes

1. "Roots" is the appellation given to a popular type of theatre production which proliferates in Jamaica. These productions rely on innuendo, usually sexual, explicit physicality, abandoned in style and intention. Scripts tend to be repetitious and not very literary.
2. Penny Carballo-Smith, a U.K. based Trinidadian, is executive director of Future Think, a Not for Profit focused on up-skilling marginalised communities in the UK and the Caribbean (www.futurethink.info).

Source: "Blood and Fire – Jamaica Political History", *World Magazine Jamaica*, 18 October 2013.

CHAPTER THIRTEEN: DIRECTORS

The Barn was host to many excellent directors, although sometimes the unschooled were difficult to restrain. Barbara Lee McCalla, who over the years was a vibrant actor, happened to be directed by men as disparate as Henk Tjon, Dennis Scott, Trevor Rhone and Lloyd Reckord. She framed a now instantly recognizable phrase: "Oh yes, he was of the push-me, pull-me school of directing."

She then continued: "Dennis Scott is high on my list as the most sympathetic, talented, caring director of them all. No pushing, no pulling."

Trevor Nairne also encouraged serious, established theatre directors to get involved.

Lloyd Reckord (1929-2015), one of Jamaica's most distinguished directors, worked in the theatre no fewer than six times during this period, presenting more challenging plays than were beginning to be the norm. He was always a family man who avidly supported his brother Barry's work[1] resulting in many fine collaborations in theatre and television in Jamaica, but more extensively in Britain, where they both experienced their finest hours. Recently, the first interracial kiss on television anywhere in the world was "rediscovered" in the archives of the British Film Institute. This now famous kiss featured Lloyd Reckord and Elizabeth McLennan in an adaptation of Barry Reckord's *You in your Small Corner*, which had been made into a television film after it's success at the Royal Court Theatre in London.

His niece, Margaret Bernal, wrote this appreciation after his death:

Lloyd Reckord's totally uncompromising stance when it came to matters of sensibility, taste, quality and cultural interpretation was well known. In some quarters he was referred to as Mr. Serious Theatre, with a definite English upperclass pronunciation of the Serious… of course! Perhaps as a result of this critical prowess, many fine, challenging plays, films, television and radio productions which have enhanced and enlightened the understanding and appreciation would never have seen the light of day.

Lloyd was not an easy man to get on with. He had no time to waste and suffered fools not at all. However, he was generous with his time when he approved of the project or person who needed his help.

This is very true. He approved of Basil Dawkins and directed two of his plays at The Barn. In 1986, there was *Champagne and Sky Juice* with Jamaican theatre royalty, Leonie Forbes and Charles Hyatt. This was one of Basil's most successful early plays. In 1994, Lloyd also directed Basil's *Power Play*.

The Reckord family is a very closely knit unit, supporting each other in a way remarkable and unusual in Jamaican theatre. In 1988, Lloyd, under the auspices of the National Theatre Trust, produced and directed his brother Barry's *Sugar D*, making this the only Barry Reckord play to have been staged at The Barn.

In 1993, a politically difficult play, *One of Our Sons is Missing*, by Trinidadian writer Godfrey Sealy,[2] who was himself to die of Aids at the age of 46, was directed by Lloyd Reckord at The Barn. This was a hard-hitting, confrontational work, set in 1988, and demanding a reality check from both family and community to come to terms with the existence of the killer in our midst. *One of Our Sons is Missing* exposes the fear and prejudice that accompanied the arrival of HIV/AIDS in a family's once safe world – a demanding play with a questioning take on gender politics at its heart.

Neil Simon, perhaps surprisingly, turns up under the Lloyd Reckord directorial banner with *Hotel Suite*, in August 1997. Produced by Sydney Reid, Lloyd Reckord not only directed this comedy, but was a member of the cast, working alongside Dervan Malcolm, Fae Ellington, Denise Hunt, Pearl McFarlane, Teddy Price and Paul Skeen.

The final play Lloyd Reckord directed at The Barn in 2002 was African American Marcia Leslie's *The Trial of One Short Sighted Black Woman*, which he had been introduced to at the National Black Theatre Festival in Winston Salem, North Carolina. This production made theatrical waves with its unusual format and, not least, the cast of grand dames: Kathy Owen and Richille Bellamy (as Victoria, the short-sighted woman), Jean Small (as the prosecutor), Amina Blackwood Meeks (as the defence attorney) and Jean Rhone and Tricia Spence (as Mammy Louise and Safreeta, respectively and Andrew Brodber (who played five characters). This play about racism in the USA, as a Barn Production, ended up with five Actor Boy Awards: Best Production, Best Director, Best Actress, Best Supporting Actor, and Best Drama.[3]

Lloyd Reckord died in 2015, aged 86:

There was also Pablo Hoilett who made his directing debut at The Barn with *Wipe That Smile*. Pablo was eminence gris at the Haining Road Theatre Place until its recent untimely closure. Hoilett directed

Dorothy Cunningham and Munair Zacca in *Lotto*

Alwin Bully's *Nite Box*

three other plays at The Barn. This included *Deloris* (1991) by John Bethencourt, one of his favourite playwrights to judge from the number of plays and adaptations of this Brazilian playwright's work he has been associated with, and in 1995 Aston Cooke's first work at The Barn, *Jamaica Rundown*, and finally in 2005 his own play, *When The Cat's Away*.

Single-minded producers who did not write or act were rare. A now legendary producer who stepped up to the plate was Ed Wallace, certainly a name to be reckoned with in the late 1970s as a wily producer of theatrical fare which had a weather eye on the box office. No bad thing, as there was now some competition from newly emerging theatre producers and venues. One of the two Ed Wallace productions at The Barn was *Labour Ward* by Lloyd Brown in 1979, directed by Keith Noel in his debut Barn appearance, introducing both Dorothy Cunningham and Alwyn Scott, both now eminent senior members of Jamaica's theatrical role of honour. *Labour Ward* was Alwyn Scott's first ever commercial theatre project. He was only nineteen and remembers The Barn and the play fondly.

Keith Noel went on to direct five more plays at The Barn over the space of two decades, between the years 1979-1999. *Labour Ward* in 1979 was followed in 1982 by Patrick Brown's *Cornflakes* and Basil Dawkins' *Parson and Mrs. Jones*. In 1985 he directed Hugh King's *Starting Over*, and finally in 1999, *Deportee Round 2* by Ginger Knight.

Alwin Bully, from the island of Dominica, became a well known and respected member of the Jamaican theatre fraternity following his arrival in Jamaica in 1987 to take up a post with UNESCO. His *Nite Box* was premiered at The Barn in 1993. He subscribes to the notion that The Barn's role in the story of Jamaican Theatre needs proper documentation and offered this observation:

> I thought it an honour to have my play on at The Barn. The fame of that space had reached me long before I came to live in Jamaica in 1987, and I had actually attended some memorable performances there in the early 70s when visiting Jamaica as President of the UWI Cave Hill Campus Guild of Undergraduates... The Barn had a warmth and intimacy that gave audiences a most intense theatre experience that has never quite been replicated in other Jamaican spaces. It had the magical ability to draw people into the heart of a story and send them home dazed and transformed through having been there. I think that's what good theatre is all about.

The Barn did not have a reputation for hosting visiting productions from outside the island, but on one occasion in 1989, the Guyanese company

Dem Two were invited to perform their socio-political revue *Dem Two: A Caribbean Experience,* stage-managed and facilitated by Munair Zacca. This production adhered to the collaborative production principle. There were three members of this company, all of whom have made important contributions to Caribbean theatre. Henry Muttoo[5] as designer par excellence, Marc Matthews,6 who worked successfully in England for many years, and Ken Corsbie[7] whose work is cherished in Guyana. Guyanese playwright Michael Gilkes (the author of *Couvade*) was also associated with this company.

Endnotes

1. Barry Reckord (1926-2011). Born in Kingston, Barry Reckord spent almost all of his adult life in the UK, but returned to Jamaica shortly before his death. His plays included *Della, Flesh to a Tiger, You in Your Small Corner, Skyvers, Don't Gas the Blacks, A Liberated Woman* and a book of reportage, *Does Fidel Eat More Than Your Father?* Three of his plays were published as *For the Reckord*, edited by Yvonne Brewster (London: Oberon, 2011). See Margaret Busby, "Barry Reckord: Obituary", *The Guardian* (UK) 16 Jan. 2012.

2. Godfrey Sealy (1960-2006). His other plays include *Home Sweet Home* (1991) and Angel (2004). *One of Our Sons is Missing* was published in *Champions of the Gayelle: You Can Lead a Horse to Water and Other Plays* (London: McMillan Caribbean, 2005).

3. A Michael Reckord footnote: His (Lloyd Reckord's) letter in the programme to potential supporters of "quality theatre," stated that in a theatrical climate which encouraged our writers "to write not better but more sensational plays" hoping to attract "mass audiences," the NTT was seeking "to revive quality theatre, set it on a solid foundation and make it viable."

4. Henry Muttoo, actor, director and theatre designer, left Guyana some time in the 1970s and settled in the Cayman Islands, where he became the artistic director of the Cayman National Cultural Foundation. He is the author of a book on Cayman art, *My Markings*.

5. Marc Matthews moved from Guyana to London in the 1970s. He is the author of two poetry collections: *Guyana My Altar* (1987), which won the Guyana Prize, and *A Season of Sometimes* (Peepal Tree, 1992).

6. Ken Corsbie was one of the founders of the Georgetown based Theatre Guild. He was a scriptwriter for a 13-part TV series in

Trinidad, *Caribbean Eye*, with Banyan Studios. He is the author of *Theatre in the Caribbean* (1983). See Roxan Kinas, "Mister Theatre: Ken Corsbie", *Caribbean Beat*, Issue 6, 1993.

7. Michael Gilkes (1933-) is a poet, dramatist, critic and pioneer of audio-visual presentations in Caribbean arts. His plays *Couvade and A Pleasant Career* are in the Peepal Tree Caribbean Modern Classics series, and his poetry collection, *Joanstown and Other Poems* was published in 2002, and won the Guyana Prize. His critical work includes *Wilson Harris and the Caribbean Novel* (1975). He left Guyana in 1961, worked for many years at Cave Hill, UWI, Barbados and currently lives in Bermuda.

CHAPTER FOURTEEN: THE PROLIFIC BASIL DAWKINS

Basil Dawkins is Jamaica's most prolific playwright:[1] he produced his first play, *Flatmate* in 1980 at The Barn and became an important contributor to this theatre's success, producing eleven production between the years 1980 and 2001. Alwyn Scott says that in *Flatmate* he fell in love with the people of theatre for their example of selflessness in getting a show ready to open. "That was real teamwork! The absolute thrill I felt on opening night and the encouragement of the entire team will always stay with me!" Basil himself remembers:

My first play *Flatmate* won a Bronze Medal in Festival in 1978, but I couldn't find anybody to produce the play or collaborate with me in any form or fashion to put the play on a stage. I was basically locked out of the system. I was to discover back then a harsh truth, which nobody is going to corroborate, yet it was my reality: when you are a black boy from the country and nobody knows your father, you didn't come up through pantomime, you didn't train in England and you didn't go to school with anybody big or were known by the elite who ran things then ... well! It was The Barn that said, "Come." A lady who lived in England, who owned The Barn, said, "Let's give him a chance." I was afforded my first opportunity in theatre production, substantially by The Barn, aided and abetted by all those who told me "no", previously. They allowed me to become a producer as well as a writer. The Barn theatre was to nurture and protect me from then – made me find my footing, learning on the fly, always knowing that when everyone else told me no, The Barn Theatre said, "Yes, let's give him a try at it."

The Barn opened up theatre in Jamaica as a popular form of entertainment and enlightenment. It wasn't closed off for upper St. Andrew folk. The humility of the setting was important; it didn't terrify anybody. I remember plays that ordinary people could relate to, plays that told our story. I don't remember a Molière but I do remember *Smile Orange* and Hugh King's *Night Work* and Carmen Tipling's *Skeleton Inside!* The Barn encouraged a fresh set of writers, young people like myself then, to continue to dig and find stories out of ourselves, and the success was reflected in the faithfulness of the following in this whisper of a theatre setting.

The Barn and I had a mutually beneficial relationship that ran over

twenty-one years and several successful productions. I am indebted to
The Barn for giving me such an opportunity.

Now follows an edited version of an interview with Basil Dawkins
whilst he was in London, overseeing the production of the London
run of his latest play, *Divorce Papers*, in the Autumn of 2015. Basil was
kind enough to find the time to respond thoughtfully to the following
questions.

YB: What brought you to writing?

BD: I am not sure at all. But let me attempt an answer with a random
collection of thoughts. I grew up the son of a mother who was a
Social Welfare Officer, later called a Community Development Officer.
She was required to create and/or produce plays using members
of these deep rural communities of marginalised rural subsistence
farmers and minimum wages field-workers at the West Indies Sugar
Company at Frome Estate (operated by Tate and Lyle of the UK).
The plays would address issues these poor folks, with a high degree
of illiteracy, had to deal in their everyday struggle at survival.

I recall scripts would come down from the Head Office in Kingston.
I specifically remembered those authored by Easton Lee. I would
as a ten year old glance through these scripts lying around the living
room or on the dining table – no particular interest, except out of
being inquisitive. I remember being particularly engaged by one
Easton Lee[1] script... It had a single name – could have been Gloria.
It was a nativity play about a baby father whose child was born
when he had used the money they had to get drunk. In his drunken
state, when he saw the mother and new born he was so moved
that he remembered the image of Mary and Jesus in the Stable. I
was moved enough to actually visit the church some evenings and
watch my mother direct the piece. I may have been curious about
the process.

What I do remember clearly is that on the night of the performance,
the community member, star of the show who played Jesus, was
nowhere to be found. The school hall was full to capacity; everybody
had come out to see this upright community man, church elder
and village lawyer play a drunk! When it finally hit that he was
really nowhere to be found, panic started to set in – not about the
missing actor – but about what would happen to all the people
who paid their sixpence for children and shilling for adults. The
church needed the money for the perpetual church building fund.
Remember, people had come very early, long before start time to
get preferred seating. The minutes were ticking way past the
announced starting time. Panic and pandemonium.

Brother (I will call him X) was finally found, drunk as a Lord.
He did not even know himself. Apparently, stage fright had gripped

Brother X and someone had advised him to just drink a flask of white rum to steady his nerves. Now, Brother X was not a rum drinker. After the first drink he started to get happy, so they gave him another to settle him down – and it did – way down almost to unconsciousness. My mother asked for his costumes, donned them and played the role. I was now hooked on reading Easton Lee's scripts.

At primary and high schools I was shy to the point of withdrawn –rural folks would call this "dark". I would be in a space having a good time with people I was familiar with, but the moment "stranger(s)" came around I was missing – to some dark corner, away from the lights. My mother frequently expressed a concern, in and out of my hearing, as to where I got this character trait from – couldn't be her – and how and by when I would grow out of it. Her immediate solution was that I should get involved in drama and acting. I thought about it but did not find the theatre programme at Mannings High School (King Henry the whichever number or *A Midsummer Night's Dream* and plays of that ilk) of any interest, certainly not enough to attract me from football or idling.

However, in my sixth form year at Mannings, a "radical" teacher came from the University of The West Indies to teach history and decided to do a play called *Chippy* [Samuel Hillary] – it had something to do with a Rastaman and the police. My friends, who ordinarily frowned at drama, were attending the rehearsals and seemed enthusiastic – which to me was astonishingly strange. When I saw the performance of *Chippy* – I decided that the next play like this I would definitely get involved – nothing more than the crowd scene though. This was not to be. The teacher responsible for *Chippy*, poor Mr. Roderick Ebanks, was fired from his job for being a radical black power revolutionary communist.

My mother was too poor to send me to university, so I was lucky to get a clerical job at the Westmoreland Resident Magistrate's Courts Office. My desire was to become a lawyer. I did not know I would be required to attend Petty Sessions Court and prosecute. Soon after I started prosecuting, I was regarded by the judge, the clerk of the courts and their deputies as somewhat gifted. I expertly mimicked the flair and facility with language I saw in those big lawyers from Kingston who came down for the Circuit Court. And I read the law books, the Archbold, the Appeal Judgements, ferociously. I was in love with the law. One day it dawned on me that all I was doing at court was acting – I was playing a role according to the scripts of the cases I was presenting. My mother was so pleased to hear reports of me standing and talking in open court. Within a short time, I was actually prosecuting at the Resident Magistrates court. After two years, I left for the University of The West Indies to pursue a degree in law on a Government Scholarship.

But not so fast.

On arriving at the University, Mona Campus, I was told my

file was mislaid between Cave Hill Campus, Barbados, which then hosted the Faculty of Law, and Mona Campus, where I was to do my first year courses. I was asked to register in the Faculty of Social Science or Arts and General Studies and do the same subjects I would have done in my first year law programme. In my first week, the University invited all freshmen to see Trevor Rhone's *Smile Orange* at the Creative Arts Centre, and as has been related elsewhere, I was transported for two hours.

I had to get involved in theatre.

I was ready.

Not quite.

Shortly after, I was asked to make up a crowd scene in a play titled *Ione* by Derek Walcott. I had one line, about four words, which I rehearsed like a professional actor would a Shakespeare sonnet. On the night of Taylor Hall's performance of *Ione*, I was excited and feeling wonderful – "If Mamma could only see me now" – in costume and all. On stage, in front of the full house it was overwhelming, but I was determined to make the best of that one line. It was when I heard my line being said by another actor, Joe Taffe, that I came back to reality. I had frozen blank. No awareness that the moment had come. They waited and Joe Taffe, in order to make the play continue, had said the four precious words. I don't recall now what the four words were. I went on to do about eighteen plays during my undergraduate years and was invited to become a member of the Caribbean Theatre Workshop, an experimental theatre group consisting primarily of graduates who were desirous of honing their acting skills.

On graduation, I was no longer able to be as deeply involved in acting as theatre time clashed with my 9 to 5. I wanted to at least be in touch with theatre somehow, and the only thing I could come up with was writing a play. I started writing *Flatmate* during the State of Emergency declared by the then Michael Manley Government. Restricted travel, hours of curfew and a solitary channel of television facilitated the completion of my first play. It was a phenomenal success from all angles. My second play, two years later, *Parson and Mrs. Jones*, was as much a failure as *Flatmate* was a success. It is in pursuit of righting the errors in *Parson and Mrs. Jones* and the lessons of what not to do and how it is not done, coupled with learning the business of producing plays at The Barn, that has enabled my continuation as a writer.

YB: Is there a pressure of being Jamaica's most prolific playwright?

BD: I am not sure if I am the most prolific theatre writer/producer currently in operation in Jamaica; what I do know I may be the only one operating as a one man band and doing it for so long and still surviving and being able to produce a show every year. It is pressure, which I enjoy and would miss immensely if anything were to cause a change that was not for the better – or even alleviating some of the pressure

– but writing and producing like this is what I know, do and enjoy despite the challenges. There is always the issue of coming up with the money to pay the creditors or repay the loans and pay the talents on schedule – and keep the audience year-in, year-out, still willing to pay to see the year's offering. It's hard and sometimes thankless. The knowledge that there are people who depend on you to carry on, propels, inspires and motivates.

YB: Critics are often not favourites with theatre people. Do they bother you?

BD: I have to be broad enough to deal with critics whose intention is often to tear down and destroy because of malice or some deep ulterior motive or bitterness with their own failings, lack of integrity or moral or ethical compass – but you bless them, give thanks and focus on what to write about next – how to make sure the next production, or the next performance, is better than the one before.

YB: What does a typical Basil Dawkins' year look like?

BD: I open a play on December 27 at the Little Little Theatre – we play 8 performances per week to the end of April. We kick off the overseas touring for Mothers Day (North America, Second weekend in May –Toronto or Florida) and then we are in and out of the country for several weekends depending on the demand for the work. But the international tours can go up to November, covering USA, Canada, now the UK and several territories in the Caribbean, including the USA and British Virgin Islands, Cayman and Bermuda.

During this time, when the new play is settled, about the end of January/ February, it is time to start thinking, conceptualizing, testing ideas about a new play for December 27, opening in ten months' time. The major challenges?

1. Coming up with an idea that is of interest not only to me but will find resonance and relevance among a wider public.

2. Making sure there is a story that can be structured with a beginning a middle and an end, and can be delivered to the public (taking full advantage of efficiencies in costs and other resources), with the best available actors, director and technical support team, and which will enable box office books to reflect and maintain a positive bottom line soon after opening and for the duration of the run.

3. Hope and pray that other theatre producers are not opening a new play in the season with the same general theme or treatment, or reflecting a similar genre, scope and approach, or even a similar title!

4. Finishing the script and the rewrites, at the latest by the second week of benefit performances of the new play, even though they have no idea what the new play is about, who is in it – just blind faith and relying on their previous experiences with a Basil Dawkins' play.

YB: What is a benefit performance?

BD: Theatre Benefit Nights was an instrument created by theatre producers, me among them, designed to sell the slow nights of a play to organizations with a captive market, who get fifty percent of the takings of the show in the hope that the benefiting organization will at least ensure you break even on the slow nights. But it is a two-edged instrument that has turned back to slice us now, because the market is now responding not to the production, but to the benefit entities, and if the night is not for a benefit, even what were traditionally strong nights are now sometimes well below capacity, so even strong nights are now being sold as benefits to protect from severe losses. Once it is a benefit performance, half the potential income goes to the benefit organization, and the producer is forced to meet the myriad of costs from the fifty percent of the proceeds, and must still pay to advertise and promote direct expenses and other indirect expenses out of the take, and still make a profit. It worked beautifully when slow nights were Tuesdays to Thursdays, but it has now come to the point where slow nights – without a benefit – can be any and each night.

YB: Apart from the annual show opening in late December and running until the Spring, do you produce anything else in Jamaica during the year?

BD: In the ordinary course of the year I also do a short season of ten performances of an old audience favourite Basil Dawkins play at the Little Theatre.[2]

Basil Dawkins, like Ginger Knight, is always at pains to elaborate on Trevor Rhone's influence on his work. Trevor was a vibrant writer of prose and Basil Dawkins treasures this note:

Deko Dawkins – like Mohamed Ali – we are the greatest. – Let no man break your spirit – Take up your pen and write. Liberate the creative imagination of your people. TDR.

Endnotes

1. Easton Lee (1931-) is a poet, dramatist, actor, theologian and theatre director. His Christian-themed plays include *Once in a Manger*, *On the Third Day* and *They That Mourn*. His collection of poetry, *From Behind the Counter* (1999) reflects his Chinese-Jamaican rural background, as does his short story collection, *Run Big 'Fraid* (2008).

2. Basil Dawkins' plays were seen on The Barn stage eleven times over a period of two decades (1980-2000)

CHAPTER FIFTEEN: APRES NAIRNE, THE BEGINNING OF THE END

Although the initial Theatre 77 objective of encouraging first-time writers and producing cutting-edge, experimental work was still important, with the departure of Trevor Nairne in 1996 from the artistic overview, informal though it was, productions at The Barn took a different slant. Jam Biz, the production company that Nairne had founded with fellow producer Lenford Salmon, had secured a venue in New Kingston on the site where the New Kingston Drive-In had been. Their work is still to be seen there; they are very successful theatre producers in Jamaica boasting a huge following, for whom they provide an unerringly well-targeted product.

In 1996, with the decline in Mr. Murray's health, my sister Valerie Chuck now managed the operation, which in all honesty became little more than a receiving venue. This was not in keeping with the objectives of the place. She found that balancing the books, although always a significant factor, became the overwhelming consideration, as some producers did not appreciate the necessity of paying their bills. The mounting deficit made it increasingly difficult to continue with a project which relied on fair play from hirers of the venue in the light of the fact that it received no public subsidy whatsoever.

Over the years, the operation had been subsidised by me somewhat, when productions, which promised a lot, delivered little. However, to continue subsidising plays that I had little regard for, seemed an effort or affront too far. For the most part, producers in general had become, understandably, much less interested in experimental work and many catered primarily to the easy laugh, using the smallest casts. I still held fast to the instructions that Hamlet gave to the players in the play performed to "catch the conscience of the King":

> ... for anything so overdone is from the purpose of playing, whose end, both at the first and now, was and is, to hold, as 'twere, the mirror up to nature [...] Now this overdone [...] though it make the unskilful laugh, cannot but make the judicious grieve... (*Hamlet*, Act III, Scene II).

Michael Reckord, long time theatre critic at *The Gleaner*, saw the writing on the wall:

> In October 1999, *Brother Desmond*, a roots play by Michael Denton, was produced by Palz Production at The Barn. It was directed by Joshua "Tommy" Tomlin. My *Gleaner* review noted that it had been touring Jamaica for a couple of years and that The Barn provided an unlikely resting place for it. I continued: "If memory serves me right, that venue, one of the most popular theatres in the island, has never before housed a roots production."

Brother Desmond did not do well at The Barn. It was of course the wrong venue for this type of production. Nor were many of the other productions at the theatre at this time commercial successes: the old audiences were wary and the audiences for the new fare on offer were not wholly enticed or impressed.

As a recipient of generous public subsidy in the United Kingdom for work which was rarely, if ever, highly commercial, I keenly appreciated the value of subsidy in situations that needed it. But as a private individual, I felt I had at least to consider the work worthwhile to fund it. To be honest, much on offer did not pass that quality test. It still took at least a decade to finally "pull the plug". Sentiment overruled common sense. Inevitably, let's say The Barn succumbed to market forces, changing preferences. The Barn had to go.

In this interim, many theatre lovers came up with ideas for the rehabilitation of the fabric of the place. Robin Baston, architect and important senior theatre person in the island, spent valuable time preparing a proposal intended to rescue the place, but with one thing and another, mainly the small matter of securing the funding to put these grand ideas into action, this did not work out. Bobb Kerr authored a similar proposal, but this too failed the financial acid test.

My sister, Valerie Chuck, observed:

> This small theatre set out in its infancy in the dying years of the 1960s to provide support, a home and a space for new challenging theatrical works, principally from the Jamaican perspective. While modern African American classics, for example *The Trial of One Short-Sighted Black Woman*, presented at the theatre in 2002, directed by Lloyd Reckord for the Jamaica National Trust, and impressively cast, added much needed gravitas to the small stage, providing excellent food for thought, this was a singular though valuable experience in this time in the life of The Barn.

If, as has been argued, certain years in the life of an theatrical organisa-tion reveal an overwhelming identification with a particular playwright, this period belongs to Aston Cooke, who to all intents and purposes dominated it. He found The Barn to be:

> a perfect little starter stage for most of us low-budget productions with huge dreams. We all had fun at The Barn, great stage and wonderful cozy environment. Mr. Murray, our Uncle, made us feel at home. I started in 1995 (*Jamaica Rundown*) so that would be 10 years… a decade at The Barn![1]

Productions written by Paul Beal also made something of a mark. In an interview with the online arts magazine, *Tallawah*, he confessed that as a high schooler he thought of himself a communist because he had read Karl Marx's *Das Kapital*. Later, all he said in relation to his experience at The Barn was:

> I staged 3 plays at The Barn Theatre back in 2004-2005… *Did Mama Know?*, *Unda Mi Nose 3* and *Pastor Hoodini*. All plays did fairly well… The experience at The Barn was good for me… The name of the company that staged the plays is Happy Island Productions Limited.

Ginger Knight, erstwhile student of Trevor Rhone in the 1970s, pro-duced two plays at The Barn early in the new century, some three decades after he had been allowed to watch fifty-two performances of *Smile Orange*. He wrote *Part Time Lover* (2002) and *Underwriters Undercover* (2004). Both are morality plays with a strong Christian ethic running through them, in a phrase: *the wages of sin is prison*.

Despite of some rather substandard, trite, unsuitable works presented, this final period of The Barn's existence makes an interesting social point. A few revivals of older classics, Rhone's *Old Story Time* and Dawkins' *Couples*, were programmed. Not much new, not much cutting edge, rather a place to resurrect old successes that still had some life in them. It was flogging dead horses and making bids for a type of audience that resisted the need for thought-provoking theatre, rather preferring to see the roots not the flowers. The Barn ended its days in March 2015 with a Jamaican revue: *Jamaica2Rahtid* by the faithful Aston Cooke.

There had been other considerations. Louis Marriott's uncensored account recalls a particularly unpleasant example of bureaucracy to which The Barn was subjected. This proved to be the first nail in its coffin. Louis Marriott records:

A memorable event relating to that production (*Jamaica in the year 2000*[2]) was the bull-in-a-china-shop antics of the KSAC Town Clerk, Errol Greene, who came ego-tripping to The Barn with JBC reporter Naomie Francis and camera crew in tow. Their story was about breaches of the KSAC's entertainment licensing regulations. Without mentioning The Barn, they cunningly used as their backdrop the front of the theatre, which every playgoer would recognise and conjured up the spectre of a theatre engulfed in flames and smoke with scores in the audience being cremated alive.

The most wicked aspect of their mischief was that they exclusively targeted The Barn, when Valerie Chuck was the most compliant of all theatre administrators in their municipality. My recollection is that she did the necessary paper work and paid her annual licence fee in June 1999, covering The Barn until June 2000. Then along came the Minister of Local Government, Arnold "Scree" Bertram, amending the regulations in September 1999, for all parish councils to follow thereafter. After the visit of these monsters, ticket sales for my production, which started very promisingly, nose-dived, so I suffered the first blow while The Barn suffered in the short, medium and long terms. Many persons who knew nothing of Errol Greene before, including myself, at once knew who he was and what he stood for.

Valerie Chuck had indeed overseen the most stringent enforcement of fire regulations by the authorities. When they were carried out at The Barn, in punctilious detail, at great expense, they resulted in a reduction in the seating of twenty seats. In a theatre that had previously seated one hundred and forty-four persons, this reduction of nearly one sixth of the seating capacity was a significant financial disincentive. Some producers found fewer seats uneconomic, and one must not forget the growing competition which the numerous other small independent theatre spaces – such as Center Stage, The New Kingston Theatre, and the Little Little Theatre – provided. Many of these now attracted the patronage of producers such as Basil Dawkins and Patrick Brown, who virtually abandoned The Barn as a venue.

Recently, in January 2016, I happened to find myself in a long queue waiting patiently to ascend the steps into the main auditorium of the Creative Arts Centre on the Mona campus of the University of the West Indies. There was some uncomfortable fidgeting, but the audience members waiting to get in were very patient and respectful. Overheard conversations alluded to the difficulty of access to this theatre as there were no ramps and the steps were uneven. When a disabled patron had been helped from his wheelchair, gently assisted up the stairs and finally into an aisle seat, he was understandably very overwrought, and the queuing punters embarrassed. Access at this venue remains exactly as it was in 2000 when the powers that be were threatening The Barn. I guess "duppy know who to frighten."[3]

Endnotes

1. Aston Cooke's revue, *Jamaica2 Rathid* was the final production on The Barn stage.
2. This work by Louis Marriott heralded the new century at The Barn.
3. Duppy is a Jamaican ghost. This old Jamaican saying suggests the wisdom of choosing an opponent who is small, vulnerable, unimportant.

CHAPTER SIXTEEN: POSTMORTEM

In 1966, the old garage of 5 Oxford Road had morphed into an small theatrical venue, out of necessity (and a giant dollop of imagination). There had been nowhere suitable or accessible for the young, idealistic group of thespians to practice their art, try out their ideas, earn their right to fail. This became known as The Barn Theatre. For the next forty years, some one hundred and twenty full-blown productions were mounted on its stage, including classics such as *Remembrance* by Derek Walcott, Strindberg's *The Father* and *What the Butler Saw* by Joe Orton.

The vast majority, some seventy-five percent of the plays produced, however, were new plays by Jamaican playwrights – a noble record by any standard. A great number of playwrights, directors and actors cut their teeth at this venue, many going on to become household names in Jamaica, at least. These include Trevor Rhone, Dennis Scott, Munair Zacca, Grace McGhie, Carmen Tipling, Stafford Ashani, Trevor Nairne, Patrick Brown, Teddy Price, Basil Dawkins…

When news of the sale of The Barn filtered through, Tanya Batson Savage of the *Gleaner* was doing a story on the need to upgrade theatrical facilities in Jamaica and wanted to use the sale of The Barn as a launching pad. She asked straightforward questions to which I gave straightforward answers. See Appendix 3.

It was not difficult to find a buyer for 5 Oxford Road. I try not to drive past the flattened place, which is now an in-bond car warehouse for one of Jamaica's wealthy outfits. I wonder if, when the big office block, or whatever they decide to build there goes up, the owners will pay any tribute to what stood there for so long, and its influence in Jamaica's creative industries. Time will tell.

Did Sydney Hibbert's original vision of a professional theatre enterprise in Jamaica by 1977 become a reality? Perhaps the thinking was not overly precise, perhaps not taking fully into account the lack of appreciation that he and others, who were trained in the theatre arts, would receive from the powerful clique of movers and shakers, who, at the time, controlled the tastes and the product.

Also, did professional theatre merely mean getting paid for work done, whether literary, technical or interpretive? Could one be partially professional? Semi-professional? At the time, perhaps insufficiently detailed thought was given to exactly what "professional" meant. Nevertheless, for those of us involved who had been trained in the theatre arts, one principal objective was to generate, eventually, a personal income, a living wage, while honourably practising, to the best of our ability, the work we had been trained to do.

An analysis of the first twelve years suggests that professionalism of a sort did exist. For the first three years the work was executed efficiently, but was, in truth, a kind of elevated amateur affair. Because there was so little audience revenue, choices had to be made: only the discipline of writing was always recompensed.

We had learned the hard way that without the play, there was no playing. However, at this stage, actors did not get paid, nor did designers or technicians: they all continued to have "day" jobs. It was 1968 before these workers were paid anything at all, and then it was negligible, per performance, never for rehearsals. I believe this practice of non-remuneration for the most important aspect of the work, the rehearsal, remains widespread in Jamaica today, despite an ever-growing number of theatre professionals who no longer have the "day" job, who earn very respectable sums from their work in local theatre. However, the ever-increasing dependence on overseas tours to make earnings truly worthwhile should not be ignored.

Amongst those individuals who were involved in The Barn at the outset, it could be said that two members of the original seven became full-time legitimate theatre professionals, working in Jamaica, from the beginning of the nineteen-seventies. One should remember that the founding aspiration was to be able to practice theatre professionally, *in Jamaica*, by 1977. By then, Trevor Rhone and Munair Zacca had to all intents and purposes become real theatre professionals – meaning that they existed principally on the proceeds from theatre and theatre-related work in Jamaica. This was now the day job.

In the case of Patricia Priestley, Billy Woung and Grace Lannaman, it is true to say that none followed theatre as a life-discipline. However, the two remaining members of the founding seven, Sydney Hibbert and Yvonne Jones Brewster did make lives in theatre, though outside Jamaica. We find that after leaving Jamaica in the 1970s, founder member Sydney Hibbert worked extensively in theatre, acting, directing and writing, not in Jamaica, but in the United States where he spent most of his professional life, twice winning, in 1983 and 1986, the Los Angeles Drama League award.[1]

Similarly, I have worked professionally in theatre for the past forty-five years, but very seldom in Jamaica. Nearly all of my work has taken place in The United States, Nigeria and Europe and principally in the United Kingdom where I founded the Talawa Theatre Company in 1985, which still enjoys a stalwart reputation as an important, well-funded, black-led producing theatre organisation.

In present day Jamaica, the number of professional actors, directors, designers and producers is markedly greater than half a century ago. The production of plays is prolific, there are audiences mesmerised by the comedic (times are hard and it's better to laugh than to cry, as the saying goes) and the monetary gains are substantial. Perhaps this development was inevitable in an environment desperate for financial freedom from those foreign forces (the IMF) who were calling in the chips of massively careless government expenditure, making the term "third world" a reality for the more unfortunate citizens. Only philosophers might now see a valid place for "serious" theatre in Jamaica.

By contrast, a tenet that our founding group held dear, we believed that our practice should provide, encourage and promote work that was worth-while, serious and principled. Posterity may judge this to have been achieved for a number of years. The Barn did open up, instigate and fashion good quality professional (and that's the key word always) theatre for Jamaicans who had grown up thinking that the local Pantomime, and Sunday morning Bim and Bam (whiteface stand-up comedy à la Jolson) shows at the Ward was all that theatre had to offer. Even if our approach could be accused of being arrogant, haphazard and personality-led, it was certainly also broad and ambitious. It proved a whetstone for the change of profile of the general theatre-going, ticket-buying demographic from an uptown, privileged, often expatriate audience, to a Jamaican public that was eager to see their own lives reflected on stage.

For a number of its final years, The Barn was host to an eclectic mix of productions. The theatre now needed to pay its way: the ongoing subsidy from my family and myself had to end. There was, and still is, no public subsidy for theatre in Jamaica and it is doubtful if there ever will be any in the foreseeable future.

Inevitably, it may be said The Barn did succumb to market forces. Ultimately, a new kind of crowd-pleasing product won the day.

Will there be a successor to The Barn? Is there a need for such a thing?

In 2005, when The Barn brought down the final curtain, I asked this question of four people who had been intimately involved with the fortunes of The Barn Theatre. Here are the responses given then:

Basil Dawkins said:

> I'm starting to panic that the life-span of the small theatre spaces is now threatened. We need to move forward to a position where we begin to assess not only the aesthetics but the economic opportunities which theatre can provide, if we aspire to become the theatrical capital of the Caribbean region. I am saddened that a society which allows the Ward Theatre to rot, might not take up the challenge. However, I feel sure that sufficient sensitivity exists in the country to make it happen.

Trevor Nairne:

> Theatre in Jamaica is not about to turn back. We are heading for a major place in the cultural industries of this country. Jamaican theatre has had good and successful diasporic exposure and the experience learned at The Barn of managing, producing, writing the work is a basis of this new trend.

Munair Zacca:

> I don't know if I am that enthusiastic about the future of theatre in Jamaica. The audiences for anything not predigested, predictable, with big, crowd-pulling comedy names as the attraction, have shrunk considerably. Tickets for benefit performances are sold out and yet you find the auditorium half empty, as people buy the tickets to support a cause but are not interested in the less banal plays. I will make an analogy with reggae, which descended into dance hall. Similarly, theatre has descended into Roots and Serial. Selah!

Now, a decade later, it may be enlightening to ask whether there was a need and if so what now constitutes the modern contemporary successor. Has the world of theatre changed? And for the better? Or what…?

So what about the "Vaulting Ambition" of the title? Did we o'er leap ourselves? Did we "fall on the other side"? As there are currently so few Jamaican-grown productions that appear to strive for the aims and objectives which the founder members of The Barn held so dear and hoped to perpetuate, then perhaps it is sadly correct to suggest that the title is tough but accurate.

But finally, a word from Trevor Rhone:[2]

One of the important decisions we made at The Barn was to take off a play which was raking it in at the Box Office, but which no longer gave us any joy. Do you remember that, Yvonne?

… i think i told u 'bout the time i had to do the minor op on the back of

my head – and the nurse say to me in preparation for the trauma, "take ur
clothes off mr. rhone – then put this on" – a little green skiff – brewsta, a
took off me shirt and put on the skiff. the wretched nurse insisted i take all
my clothes off – i tried explaining to her that the operation was on the back
of my head – so i didn't see why i had to take my underwear off. she
wouldn't listen to reason so there i was dressed in this little skiff with the
whole of the back open an de whole of mi batty out a door. i asked if she had
a pin to – y'know – the back of the skiff so i wouldn't be so exposed. 'pins
are not allowed mr. rhone'. masking tape even i insisted. finally, brewsta,
a little piece of masking tape held my dignity together. kept me intact as i
set out down the long corridor to the place of my ordeal. Two steps was all
it took brewster and it all came asunder. I now had a masking tape tail and
the whole of mi batty out a door for all the world to see. That moment
Brewsta was a moment of great revelation – me trevor rhone – big
playwright – international an all with the whole of him batty out a door
walking down a long breezy corridor. it all became clear to me – i saw myself
in the scheme of things – a mere fragile mortal. all the pretence and the
hostility and the grasping and the deception and the greed and the need for
power all comes to naught – like a puff of smoke in the wind.

so brewsta, sorry there is no working with u on this one, and that fills me
with a sadness, but there will be other corridors – other times coz u like me
are children of the gods and our destinies and pathways are one.

in love, faith, trust & openness

tdr1 mister.

Endnotes

1. Hibbert's publication *Anansi and Muntu: a Caribbean Soul in Exile*,
   grew from dramatic presentations of his work staged with three
   musicians in New York and Los Angeles as early as 1976.
2. In an email to Yvonne Brewster shortly before his death:
   "I don't think downright we must even blame our audiences. Why
   should the ticket purchasing public which remains to my mind so
   loyal, bear criticism for what is perceived as lack of theatre spaces.
   It's the duty of those of you earn their living from theatre to lobby,
   to invest, to pay their bills on time, to provide the safe venues for
   their work.

   They must make sure that Public (read Governmental again) funds
   are available to subsidize their art and their creative endeavours. The
   paying public will always support them if they get it right."

APPENDIX ONE: PLAYWRIGHTS AT THE BARN

NAME	PRODUCTION	NATIONALITY	YEAR
ABBENSETTS, Michael	Sweet Talk	Guyanese	1977
ALBEE, Edward	Zoo Story	American	1965
ASHANI, Stafford	The Quickie	Jamaican	1975
	Foreign Mind		1989
BEALE, Paul O	Under Mi Nose	Jamaican	2003
	Did Mama Know?		2004
	Pastor Hoodini		2005
BETHENCOURT, John	Deloris	Brazilian	1991
BINNS et al	I'm Human Right?	British/Jamaican	1968
BROWN, Lloyd	Labour Ward	Jamaican	1979
BROWN, Patrick	Cornflakes	Jamaican	1982
	Friends		1987
	Guava Jelly		1989
	Yard 89		1989
	Yard 90		1990
	December		1991
	Puppy Love		1996
BULLINS, Edward	Electronic Nigger	American	1967
BULLY, Alwin	Nite Box	Dominican	1993
CLARKE, Joey	King of the Hill	British	1993
	Making a Killing		2004
COOKE, Aston	Jamaica Pepperpot	Jamaican	1996
	Front Room		1998
	Country Duppy		2000
	Kiss Mi Neck		2001
	Single Entry		2003
	Jamaica 2 Rahtid		2005
COONEY, Ray	Run For Your Wife	British	1995
CROSSKILL, Daryll	It's Not My Fault Baby	British	1967
CUMPER, Patricia	Buss Out	Jamaican	1989
DAILEY SALMON, Andrea	Death Row	Jamaican	2002
DAWKINS, Basil	Flat Mate	Jamaican	1980
	Parson and Mrs Jones		1982
	Couples		1984
	Champagne and Sky Juice		1986
	Power Play		1994
	Couples		1994
	Toy Boy		1995
	Champagne and Sky Juice		1988
	Couples		2000
	Couples		2001

DEM TWO COMPANY	Dem Two	Guyanese	1989
DENTON, Michael	Brother Desmond	Jamaican	2005
HENRY, Edward	See Mama	Jamaican	1972
HERON, David	Ecstacy	Jamaican	1994
HILARY. Sam	Koo Koo	Jamaican	1968
HOILETTE, Pablo	When The Cat's Away	Jamaican	2005
HOPKINSON, Slade	Sala	Guyanese	1974
HUGHES, Langston	Ask Your Mama	American	1966
KING, Hugh	Jonathan Digby	Jamaican	1977
	Night Work		1979
	Killer		1980
	Greasy Spoon		1982
	Starting Over		1985
	Undercover Lover		1986/1990
	Ramrod		1987
KNIGHT, Ginger	Deportee Round 2	Jamaican	1999
	Part-time Lover		2002
	Underwriters Undercover		2004
LESLIE, Marcia L	Trial of One Short Sighted Black Woman	American	2002
MAIR, Oliver	Dat Ting	Jamaican	1999
	Tek Dat Ting Mek Laugh		2000
MAIS, Roger	Rolando and Rosamund	Jamaican	1967
MARRIOT, Louis	One Stop Driver	Jamaican	1986
	Office Case		1986
	Jamaica in the Year 2000		2000
MARTIN, Jackson	It's Not My Fault Baby	Jamaican	1967
MAXWELL, Ken	Please	Jamaican	1970
MILNER, Roger	How's the World Treating You?	British	1966
ORTON, Joe	What the Butler Saw	British	1971
OSBOURNE, Kay	Wipe That Smile	Jamaican	1978
PINTER, Harold	The Collection	British	1968
RECORD, Barry	Sugar D	Jamaican	1988
RHONE, Trevor	Look Two	Jamaican	1967
	It's Not My Fault Baby		1967
	Yes Mama		1968
	The Gadget		1970
	Smile Orange		1971
	Sleeper		1971
	Comic Strip		1973
	Schools Out		1974
	Two Can Play		1982
	The Game		1985
	One Stop Driver		1988
	Smile Orange		1992
	Old Story Time		1999

	Bellas Gate Boy		2003
	Positive		2005
SAUNDERS, James	Neighbours	British	1967
SHAKESPEARE, William	Midsummer Nights Dream	British	1971 EXCERPT
SCHOOL'S TOUR	Julius Caesar		EXCERPT
	Hamlet		EXCERPT
SCOTT, Dennis	The Inquisitors	Jamaican	1967
SEALY, Godfrey	One of Our Sons is Missing	Trinidadian	1993
SIMON, Neil	One More Time		1998
	Hotel Suite		1997
SISTREN	Bellywoman Bangarang	Jamaican	1978
	Bandoolu Version		1979
	QPH		1981
	Buss Out		1989
	Mirror Mirror		1997
SLADE, Bernard	Same Time Next Year	Canadian	1981
STRINDBERG, August	Miss Julie	Swedish	1965
	The Father		1999
TIPLING, Carmen	Straight Man	Jamaican	1974
	The Skeleton Inside		1976
TJON, Henk	Hot Flashes	Dutch	1995
TRIANO, Jose	The Criminals	Cuban	1974
WALCOTT, Derek	Rememberance	St Lucian	1979
WARNER, Earl	Man Talk	Barbadian	1996
	Jamaica 360		2003
ZACCA, Munair	Play It	Jamaican	1994
Collaborations :			
Ed Wallace/ Renee Taylor/ Joseph Bologna	Bedtime Stories		1998
Barbara Raskin/ Miriam Ba/ Jamaica Kincaid/ Jean Rhys/ Lillian Rubin	Hot Flashes		1995
Christopher Daley/ Mark Danvers/ Donald Anderson	One Pack of Crackers		2000

APPENDIX TWO: PLAYS AT THE BARN

Year	Playwright	Play	Director	Cast	Comments
1965	August Strindberg	Miss Julie	Sydney Hibbert	Yvonne Jones, Trevor Rhone, Pat Priestly, Munair Zacca.	March
1965	Edward Albee	Zoo Story	Trevor Rhone	Billy Woung, Sidney Hibbert	March
1966	Roger Milner	How's The World Treating You?	Trevor Rhone	Yvonne Jones, Pat Priestly, Billy Woung, Sidney Hibbert, Vincent McKie, Andrew Garbutt, Munair Zacca, Pam Hitchins	July
1966	Various	Poetry in Performance	George Carter	Dennis Scott, John Hearne, Basil McFarlane, Mervyn Morris	October On the Off Beat double bill with Ask Your Mama
1966	Langston Hughes	Ask Your Mama	George Carter	Cheryl Ryman, Munair Zacca, Trevor Rhone, Yvonne Jones	October On the Off Beat double bill with Poetry in Performance
1967	Trevor Rhone	Look Two	Yvonne Jones	Munair Zacca	July Xperiment V Triple bill with Rolando and Rosamund & The Inquisitors
1967	Roger Mais	Rolando and	Yvonne Jones	Lennie Little-White, Cheryl Ryman, Munair Zacca, Jean Samms	July Xperiment V Triple bill with Look Two & Inquisitors
1967	Dennis Scott	The Inquisitors	Trevor Rhone	Munair Zacca	July Xperiment V Triple bill with Rolando and Rosamund & Look two
1967	Ed Bullins	Electronic Nigger	Yvonne Jones	Coleen Kong, Stan Irons, Trevor Rhone, Jimmy Eldridge	July In the Round Double bill with Neighbours In the Round Double Bill with Electronic Nigger
1967	James Saunders	Neighbours	Yvonne Jones	Munair Zacca, Judi Crane	July In the Round Double Bill with Electronic Nigger
September 23rd 1967 Karl Parbosingh presents mural to the Barn Theatre					
1968	Trevor Rhone, Daryl Crosskill, Jackson Martin	It's Not My Fault Baby	George Carter Trevor Rhone Yvonne Jones	Melba Bennett, Eula Fraser, Roy Case, Cheryl Ryman, Trevor Rhone, Tess Thomas, Yvonne Jones, Munair Zacca	January
1968	Several Authors Graham Binns	"I'm Human Right?"	Neville Black	Raymond Hill, Melba Bennett, Pauline Cowan, Trevor Rhone, Yvonne Jones Munair Zacca, Gladstone Wilson, Cheryl Ryman	June Satirical Revue Double Bill with Yes Mama. Music by Marjorie Whylie
1968	Trevor Rhone	Yes Mama	Yvonne Jones	Cheryl Ryman, Melba Bennett, Munair Zacca, Betty Canton	June Double Bill with "I'm Human Right?"
July 19 1968 Children's Drama Classes were launched					
1967	Sam Hillary	Koo Koo	Yvonne Jones	Munair Zacca, Trevor Rhone, Elizabeth Joyce, Vincent McKie	
1968	Harold Pinter	The Collection	Yvonne Jones	Munair Zacca, Trevor Rhone, Mike Lewis, Joanna Hart	
1969 Ceramic Exhibition by Gene Pearson Back O the Barn					
1969	Trevor Rhone	The Gadget	Ancile Gloudon Trevor Rhone	Inez Hibbert, Munair Zacca, Ancile Gloudon, Patrick Lewis	July
1970	Ken Maxwell	Please	Tom Cook	Munair Zacca, Yvonne Jones, Trevor Rhone, Ken Cole, Pauline Cowan, Joanna Hart, Volier Johnson, Philip Zin, Ken Maxwell	June Satirical Revue

Year	Author	Title	Director	Cast	Notes
1971	Shakespeare	Midsummer Night's Dream; Julius Caesar; Hamlet	Sam Walters	Janet Bartley, Joanna Hart, Munair Zacca, Yvonne Jones, Trevor Rhone, Peter Ashbourne, Bim Lewis, Andrew Garbutt	February Featuring Bim Lewis as Bottom
1971	Joe Orton	What the Butler Saw	Eileen Porter	Trevor Rhone, Yvonne Jones, Munair Zacca, Janet Bartley, Andrew Garbutt, Ernest Cromwell	Set and design by Jonathan Porter. Final performance 10th April 1971
	Trevor Rhone	Sleeper	Dennis Scott	Grace McGhie, Barbara McCalla, Anna Hearne, Joe Taffe, Val Morris, Stan Irons, Keith Sasso, Natalie Thompson, Joanna Hart	June
Jean Taylor Ceramics Exhibition May 2nd 1971					
Back O' the Barn Ceramics closes down in June 1971					
Ceramics Summer Classes begin					
1971	Trevor Rhone	Smile Orange	Dennis Scott	Carl Bradshaw, Harvel Peryer, Stan Irons, Vaughn Crosskill, Grace McGhie	October. no perfs 18th December - 3rd January. Opened 2nd November. 16th August 1972, 100 performances
1973	Edward E. Henry	See Mama	Munair Zacca	Barbara McCalla, Jackson Gordon, Keith Gordon, Harry Bell, Stafford Harrison, Claudia Robinson, Leonie Forbes, Robert Morris, Sandra Redwood	January
1973	Trevor Rhone	Comic Strip	Trevor Rhone	Carl Bradshaw, Grace McGhie, Patricia Cumper, Cheryl Stuart, Roy Case, Ruth Ho Shing	Month unknown
		Comic Strip (Version 2)	Melba Bennett	Evet Hussey, Aileen Grant, Cecile Clayton, Bob Kerr	
1974	Slade Hopkinson	Sala	Dennis Scott	Christine Bell, David Carty, Grace McGhie, Teddy Price, Stan Irons, Fae Ellington	February
1974	Jose Triano	The Criminals	Munair Zacca	Anna Hearne, Hillary Nicholson, Stafford Ashani	July
1974	Trevor Rhone	School's Out	Yvonne Jones	Oliver Samuels, Bob Kerr, Brian Heap, Pauline Cowan, Vernon Derby, Glen Campbell, Vincent McKie, Calvin Foster, Harold Brady, Teddy Price, Trevor Nairne	November Now Yvonne Brewster. Closed on 23rd November.
1974	Carmen Tipling	Straight Man	Munair Zacca	Stafford Harrison, Christine Bell, Ruel Cooke, Arthur Brown	December Arthur Brown, Dennis Brown's Father
1975	Stafford Ashani	The Quickie	Munair Zacca	Aggrey Irons, Pat Lindsay, Gayman Alberba, Gabrielle Harban	
1976	Carmen Tipling	The Skeleton Inside	Dennis Scott	Grace McGhie, Honor Ford-Smith, Pauline Cowan, Trevor Nairne, Jonathan Brown, Val Morris, Howard Facey, Pat Lindsay, Cecile Clayton, Zac Henry	Closed February 1977
1977	Michael Abbensett	Sweet Talk	Munair Zacca	John Francis, Cynthia Henry, Honor Ford-Smith, Hillary Nicholson, Debbie Glanville, Claire Harris	
1977	Hugh King	The Resurrection of Jonathan Digby	Hugh King	Hugh King, Manny Wilson, Charmaine Creighton, Maureen Barton, Jane Belton, Lenroy Savory	November 90 performances
1978	Kay Osbourne	Wipe That Smile	Pablo Hoilett	Denise Oates, Ronald Goshop, Evet Hussey, Carl Bradshaw, Clive Walker, Arthur Brown	
1978	Michael Reckord	Flip Side:Death	Michael Reckord		student production

1978	Sistren	Belly Woman Bangarang	Honor Ford Smith	Beverly Elliott, Beverly Hanson, Rebecca Knowles, Barbara Gayle, Lana Finikin, Pauline Crawford, Lillian Foster, Vivette Lewis, Cerine Stephenson	Produced by Sistren Women's collective, improvisation
1978	Hugh King	Night Work		Charmaine Hemmings, Hugh King, Charmaine Creighton, John Ellis, Lenroy Savery, Peter Austin	31st December
1979	ANONYMOUS	A State of Mind	Stan Irons	Val Morris, Johnathan Brown, Carmen Clarke, Denise Oates, Marrietta Armstrong, Natalie Thompson, Rosemary Murray, Evet Hussey, Cyrene Tomlinson, Errol Palmer	June Valtran Productions
1979	Lloyd Brown	Labour Ward	Keith Noel	Marva Gallimore, Dorothy Cunningham, Delores Williams, John Francis, William Rose, Merlene McLean, Alwyn Scott	October Ed Wallace Production
1979	Honor Ford Smith	Bandoolu Version	Honor Ford Smith	Sistren Collective	
1979	Marc Connolly	Green Pastures	Norman Martin	Carl Davis, Maurice Powell, Desmond Hall, Tyrone Whyte, Hilary Lawrence	
1979	Derek Walcott	Remembrance	Trevor Nairne	Eugene Williams, Hugh Martin, Egerton Rhoden, Natalie Thompson, Baldwin Howe, Brian Heap, Gillian Nicholas, Cecile Williams	Produced by Trevor Rhone Opened 10th December 1979
1980	Basil Dawkins	Flat Mate	Keith Noel	Alwyn Scott, Ruth Ho Shing, Dorothy Cunningham, Earl Marsh, Harold Newell Jr	
1980	Hugh King	Killer	Charmaine Creighton	Eugene Dywer, Lola Hamilton, Hugh P Morrison, Rosemary Murray, Michael Everett, Hugh King, Leroy Savery, Jean Small	December
1981	Sistren Devised	QPH	Hertencer Lindsay	Sistren Company	
1981	Bernard Slade	Same Time Next Year	Bobby Ghisays	Rooney Chambers, Dawn Forrester	
1982	Patrick Brown	Cornflakes	Keith Noel	Calvin Butler, Hope Blake, Clive Anderson, Rosemary Murray	
1982	Basil Dawkins	Parson and Mrs. Jones	Keith Noel	Oscar Lee, Pauline Stone Myrie, Faye Bell	Pauline and Faye alternating
1982	Hugh King	Greasy Spoon	Keith Noel	Michael Everett, Ronald Goshop, Faith D'Aguilar, Teddy Price, Stan Irons	28th July
1982	Trevor Rhone	Two Can Play	Trevor Rhone	Barbara McCalla, Grace McGhie, Charles Hyatt, Homer Heron	
1984	Basil Dawkins	Couples	Bari Johnson	Teddy Price, Ruth Ho Shing, Barbara Harriott, Joe Taffe, Barbara McCalla, Faye Bell, Val Morris, Keith Noel	12th October
1985	Hugh King	Starting Over	Keith Noel	Totlyn Oliver, Stan Irons, Fitz Weir, Grace McGhie, Dennis Titus, Carl Matthew	November
1985	Trevor Rhone	The Game	Trevor Rhone	Munair Zacca, Sheryn Hylton, Brian Heap, Earl Marsh	
1986	Hugh King	Ramrod	Bobby Ghisays	Christine Bell, Ronald Goshop, Fitz Weir, Clive Walker, Hugh King, Henry Johnson, Manny Wilson, George Silvera	April Opened April with final week 8th July
1986	Louis Marriott	Office Chase	Louis Marriott	Glen Campbell, Christine Bell, Pearl McFarlane, Dorothy Cunningham, Carl Davis, Bagga Brown, Lenford Salmon, Louis Marriott	26th June
1986	Basil Dawkins	Champagne and Sky Juice	Lloyd Reckord	Charles Hyatt, Leonie Forbes	

1987	Patrick Brown	Friends	Trevor Nairne	Glen Campbell, Rosemary Murray, Bertina MacCaulay	8th July
	Basil Dawkins	Same Song Different Tune	Lloyd Reckord	Buddy Pouyatt, Teddy Price, Barbara McCalla, Carol Lawes, Rosemary Murray, Karen Harriott, Clive Anderson, Blaka Ellis	5th June
1988	Trevor Rhone, Louis Marriott	One Stop Driver	Charles Hyatt	Grace McGhie, Fae Ellington, Glen Campbell, Peter Lloyd, Munair Zacca, Paula Munroe, Karen Harriott, Teddy Price	Musical Revue
1988	Barry Reckord	Sugar D	Lloyd Reckord	Ronald Goshop, Georgia Ellis, Bari Johnson	National Theatre Trust Production
1988	Hugh King	Undercover Lover	Hugh King	Anita Stewart, Fitz Weir, Hyacinth Brown, Richard Johnson, Henry Johnson, Hugh King, Glen Morrison	150 performances
	Ed Wallace, Renee Taylor, Joseph Bologna	Bedtime Stories	Bari Johnson	Volier Johnson, Karl Binger, Grace McGhie, Pearl McFarlane, Yolande Bramwell	
1989	Patrick Brown	Guava Jelly	Trevor Nairne	Rosemary Murray, Clive Anderson, Glen Campbell, Owen Ellis, Andrea Anderson	
1989	Pat Cumper	Buss Out	Earl Warner	Beverly Elliott, Beverly Hanson, Jean Kelly, Joy Erskine, Jerline Todd, Hillary Nicholson, Lillian Foster, Annie Blake	Produced by Sistren Women's Collective
1989	Patrick Brown	Yard 89	Trevor Nairne	Glen Campbell, Tony Hendriks, Rosie Murray, Clive Anderson, Denise Robinson, Denise Thompson, Bertina MacCauley, Andrea Haynes	Revue Produced by Better Theatre Productions
1989	Stafford Ashani	Foreign Mind	Trevor Nairne	Mizan Nunes, Paul Campbell, Baldwin Howe, Karen Harriott	Produced by: Stafford Ashani & Victor Harrison
1989	Dem Two Company from Guyana	Dem Two - A Caribbean Experience	Henry Muttoo	Ken Corsbie, Marc Mathews	Design by Henry Muttoo
1990	Patrick Brown	Yard 90	Trevor Nairne	Karen Harriott, Claudette Pious, Glen Campbell, Clive Anderson, Rosemary Murray, Karen Harriott, Clive 'Uzu' Anderson, Owen "Blacka" Ellis, Earl Marsh, Johnathan Brown	Revue Produced by Better Theatre Productions
1991	Patrick Brown	December	Trevor Nairne	Leonie Forbes, Errol Jones	Produced by Patrick Brown
1991	John Bethencourt	Deloris	Pablo Hoilett	Grace McGhie, Karl Binger, Trevor Fearon, John Jones, Hugh Martin	Brazilian playwright
1992	Trevor Rhone	Smile Orange	Trevor Nairne	Glen Campbell, Teddy Price, Lenford Salmon, Rosemary Murray, Karen Harriott, Clive 'Uzu' Anderson, Owen "Blacka" Ellis, Michael Forrest	October 21st Anniversary Production
1993	Alwin Bully	Nite Box	Alwin Bully	Mark Martin, Cathi Levi, Joey Clarke, Christine Bell, Clive Anderson, Christopher Daley, Carl Davis, Ana Harris, Lenford Salmon, Clive Duncan, Erica Brown, Jean Rhone, Laura Finikin	21st April Designed by Alwin Bully, LX/SFX by George Silvera, Managed by Sheila Graham
1993	Godfrey Sealy	One Of Our Sons Is Missing	Lloyd Reckord	Karl Binger, Claudette Pious, Clive Anderson, Norman Pottinger	15th June - August Produced by Better Theatre Productions
1993	Joey Clarke	King Of The Hill	Joey Clarke, Munair Zacca	Ruth Ho Shing, Joey Clarke, Carl Davis, Sheryl Arthurs, Madge Martin	
1994	Ray Cooney	Run For Your Wife	Trevor Nairne, Lenford Salmon	Christine Bell, Teddy Price, Clive 'Uzu' Anderson, Glen Campbell, Carl Davis, Peter Hislop, Pearl McFarlane, Marguerite Newland, Norman Pottinger, Claudette Pious, Luke Williams	15th January 1993 An adaptation of the original. Produced by Better Theatre Productions
1994	Basil Dawkins	Power Play	Lloyd Reckord	Teddy Price, Canute Fagan, Jonathan Brown, Volier Johnson, Carl Davis, Christine Bell, Pearl McFarlane	

1994	Munair Zacca	Play It	Munair Zacca	Munair Zacca, Bertina McCauley, Pablo Hoilett, Ronald Goshop, Joey Clarke, Denise Robinson	
1994	Basil Dawkins	Couples		Terry Salmon, Karen Jones, Paul Skeen, Rosemary Murray, Christine Bell, Aston Cooke, Teddy Price	
1994	David Heron	Ecstasy	Trevor Nairne	Deon Silvera, Terry Salmon, Jean Kelly White, Dino Maharaj, Chrismore Mills, Michelle Shields	Produced by Better Theatre Productions
1995	Basil Dawkins	Toy Boy	Buddy Pouyatt	Leonie Forbes, Charles Hyatt	
1995	Script adapted from separate writings by: Barbara Raskin, Miriama Ba, Jamaica Kincaid, Jean Rhys & Lillian Rubin	Hot Flashes	Henk Tjon	Leonie Forbes, Grace McGhie, Barbara McCalla, Jean Small, Marjorie Whylie, Fae Ellington	Adapted by Henk Tjon Produced by Alwin Bully
1996	Aston Cooke	Jamaica Rundown	Pablo Hoilett	Glen Campbell, Munair Zacca, Christopher Daley, Totlyn Oliver, Fleurette Harris, Tulip Reid	Revue
1996	Earl Warner	Man Talk	Earl Warner	Ralph Campbell, Bobby Clarke, Mark Danvers, Karl Binger, Tony Hendriks, Owen 'Blacka' Ellis, Russell Watson	
1996	Aston Cooke	Jamaica Pepperpot	Fabian Thomas	Christopher Daley, Vernon Derby, Steve Higgins, Michael Nicholson, Totlyn Oliver, Deon Silvera	Musical Revue Music by Grub Cooper Kwanzaa Production
1996	Patrick Brown	Puppy Love	Trevor Nairne	Marguerite Newland, Grace McGhie, Clive Anderson, Karl Binger, Amelia 'Milk' Sewell, Tessa Linton, Munair Zacca	Produced by Better Theatre Productions
1997	Neil Simon	Hotel Suite	Lloyd Reckord	Pearl McFarlane, Paul Skeen, Fae Ellington, Lloyd Reckord, Denise Hunt, Teddy Price, Dervan Malcolm	
1997	Sistren	Mirro Mirro	Jean Small	Afollo Shadae, Donnet Hines-Furzur	
1998	Neil Simon	One More Time	Patrick Brown	Deon Silvera, Glen Campbell	adapted from Neil Simon's
1998	Aston Cooke	Front Room	Michael Nicholson	Dorothy Cunningham, Deon Silvera, Terri Salmon, Dawnette Hinds, Bert Johnson, Canute Lawrence, Clifton Danvers	2nd April
1998	Basil Dawkins	Champagne and Sky Juice	Buddy Pouyatt	Grace McGhie, Ronald Goshop	2nd Production
1999	August Strindberg	The Father	Norman Rae	Leonie Forbes, Brian Heap, Rooney Chambers, Lois Kelly-Miller, Michael Daley, Neville Bramwell, Karen Seymour, Douglas McIntosh	3rd June 1999 Produced by Pauline Stone-Myrie & Norman Rae for Theatre People
1999	Ginger Knight	Deportee Round 2	Keith Noel	Ginger Knight, Christopher Ready, Ruth Knight, Dean Martin, Joy Grandison, Dayne McDonald, Joan Williams, Glendon Jarrett, Charles Knight	9th July 1999 Toured extensively in the USA
1999	David Heron	Against His Will	Trevor Nairne	Douglas Prout, Munair Zacca, Karl Binger, Karen Harriott, Margaret Young	A Jambiz Production
1999	Oliver Mair	Dat Ting	Ricardo Nichols	Calvin Morris, Rodney Campbell, Winston Rowe, Elva Ruddock, Marlon King, Carrol Gordon	
1999	Trevor Rhone	Old Story Time	Trevor Rhone	Charles Hyatt, Teddy Price, Leonie Forbes, Carrol Russell, Barbara Harriott, Calvin Foster, Carl Binger, Pauline Kerr, Alwyn Scott, Bobby Ghisays, Keith Sasso	

2000	Louis Marriott	Jamaica in the Year 2000	Louis Marriott	Christopher Daley, Denise Hunt, Sherando Ferril, Dayne McDonald	
2000	Christopher Daley, Mark Danvers, Donald Anderson	One Pack of Crackaz	Mark Danvers	Donald Anderson, Mark Danvers, Christopher Daley, Scarlett Beharie, Marcellas James, Chris McFarlane, Winston 'Ricky' Rowe	Krunch Productions
2000	Oliver Mair	Tek Dat Ting Mek Laugh	Ricardo Nicholas	Rodney Campbell, Calvin Morris, Elva Ruddock, Winston Rowe, Carrol Gordon, Marlon King	
2000	Aston Cooke	Country Duppy	Michael Nicholson	Leonie Forbes, Tulip Reid, Christopher Daley, Clifton Danvers, Peter Heslop	7th December 2000
2000	Basil Dawkins	Couples	Basil Dawkins	Christine Bell, Teddy Price, Paul Skeen, Terri Salmon	2nd Production
2001	Basil Dawkins	Couples	Buddy Pouyatt	Elizabeth Haye, Fae Ellington, Munair Zacca, Marsha Ann Hay, Paul Lindo, Paul Skeen	3rd Production
2001	Aston Cooke	Kiss Mi Neck	Michael Nicholson	Donald Anderson, Jerry Benzwick, Clifton Danvers, Fae Ellington, Terri Salmon, Gracia Thompson, Dahlia Harris	Musical Revue Music by Grub Cooper, Movement by Monica Lawrence
2002	Marcia L Leslie	Trial of One Short Sighted Black Woman	Lloyd Reckord	Kathy Owen, Rishille Bellamy, Amina Blackwood-Meeks, Dorothy Cunningham, Jean Small, Totlyn Oliver, Andrew Brodber, Khadija Fudail, Jean Rhone, Tricia Spence, Marsha-Ann Hay	National Theatre Trust Production
2002	Ginger Knight	Part Time Lover	Ginger Knight, Volier Johnson, Deon Silvera	Volier Johnson, Dayne McDonald, Ruth Knight, Marsha-Ann Hay, Deon Silvera, Charles Knight, Ginger Knight	10th May
2002	Andrea Dailey-Salmon	Death Row	Kenny Salmon	Courtney Wilson, Orville Hall, Alton Locke, Phillip Watkis, Kimberly Smith, Vanessa Baugh, Diandra Salomon, Raquel Sutherland, Hopeton Henry	
	Trevor Rhone	Bellas Gate Boy	Yvonne Brewster	Trevor Rhone, Alwyn Scott	December 2002 Set designed by Ellen Cairns
2003	Earl Warner	Jamaica 360	Earl Warner		
2003	Aston Cooke	Single Entry	Michael Nicholson	Deon Silvera, Terri Salmon, Paul Skeen, Jerry Benswick	July
2003	Paul Beale	Under Mi Nose	Paul Beale	Dayne McDonald, Donald Thompson, Dennis Hall, Tanya Graham, Donna Bucknall	Happy Island Production
2004	Paul Beale	Did Mama Know?	Paul O Beale	Belinda Reid, Junior Williams, Kerry-Ann, Dawn Nugent, Etmore Williams, Simone Bartley	Happy Island Production
2004	Ginger Knight	Underwriters Undercover	Ginger Knight	Earl Brown, Ruth Knight, Elvis Hamilton, Marsha-Ann Hay, Ginger Knight	23rd April Originally directed by E. Lloyd Napier
2004	Joey Clarke	Making A Killing	Bob Kerr	Charles Hyatt, Fae Ellington, Maylynne Walton, Paul Skeen, Monique Caesar, Canute Fagan	
2004	Kenny Salmon	Hot Pepper Sauce	Kenny Salmon	David Crossgill, Orville Hall, Diandra Salmon, Shereece Wheeler, Everaldo Creary	
2005	Paul Beale	Pastor Hoodini	Paul O Beale	Andrea Wright, Junior Williams, Dennis Hall, Paul O Beale, Antonet Fagon	Happy Island Production
2005	Trevor Rhone	Positive	Fabian Thomas	Dorothy Cunningham, Michael Nicholson, Teisha Duncan, Keneisha Bowes, Camille Davis, Robert Clarke, Christopher Gordon, Everaldo Creary	Music by Grub Cooper, Lyrics by Fabian Thomas, Choreography by Michael Holgate Joint Production of JADA and Ministry

2005	Pablo Hoilett	When The Cat's Away	Pablo Hoilett	Calvin Morris, Michael Forrest, Stephanie Ruddock, Linear Hines, Totlyn Oliver, Audrey Reid	
2005	Michael Denton	Brother Desmond	Joshua Tomlin	Joshua Tomlin, Jeffrey Williams, Francine Michelle, Nicholas Hemmings, Mytania Samuels, Autherine ?, Keisha ?	
2005	Aston Cooke	Jamaica 2 Rahtid	Michael Nicholson	Deon Silvera, Everaldo Creary, Terri Salmon, Christopher Daley, Christopher McFarlane, Dahlia Harris, Michael Nicholson	Musical Revue Music by Grub Cooper Choreography by Orville Hall

APPENDIX 3

Text of an interview with Yvonne Brewster by *Gleaner* journalist Tanya Batson Savage in 2005.

TBS: Why is The Barn being sold?

YB: I have with a sad heart sold The Barn. The reasons are many and complex, but suffice it to say that one of the major determining factors was its dire need of refurbishment which could not possibly be paid for by the rental. Also with the loud noise from Mas Camp only a few hundred yards away, the competition became too much for the single human voice. Another, possibly for me more telling reason is that I no longer felt persuaded to continue subsidizing work which was so blatantly commercial. In all modern civilized societies theatre is a necessary, but increasingly expensive commodity. More often than not, and this is not only a Jamaican phenomenon, the taste for the obvious and the banal, crowds out appreciation of the subtle and the more considered. Discussion of the important role of public (read Governmental) support and subsidy of the non-commercial arts becomes even more essential if contemporary Jamaican theatre is to rise above the obvious and leave a proud legacy. Private citizens may no longer wish to subsidize this cultural responsibility alone.

TBS: It was intended to be an experimental space, do you think it lived up to its purpose?

YB: Yes. The Barn in its heyday was always experimental. Without the luxury of experiment, theatre becomes a mere pastiche. For a time, it certainly lived up to its purpose, as the freedom to experiment it gave allowed a number of playwrights, directors, designers and even one or two poets and academics to imagine freely and act upon it. Most, if not all, of Trevor Rhone's plays cut their teeth there. Carmen Tipling, Stafford Harrison, Sistren, Dennis Scott, John Hearne, Cheryl Ryman, Basil Dawkins, Basil MacFarlane, Meryvn Morris, Lennie Littlewhite, George Carter – the list is endless – all experimented at The Barn, but times change and there hasn't been much experiment there latterly. All good things come to an end and I guess this moment was reached quite a few years ago. It was difficult, painful, but necessary to finally face up to the fact that what we did then has little or no meaning in today's Jamaican theatrical world.

TBS: When it was created, what did you imagine would become of The Barn theatre?

YB: We founded The Barn in 1965 and gave the resident company the name Theatre 77. In twelve years, we predicted there would be a fully professional theatre in Jamaica – 65 plus 12 equals 77. That was the goal which kept us, a disparate group of Jamaicans, all recently trained in England and the USA, and returning home with cultural revolution in our heads. We achieved this. I don't think we thought much about posterity and that's just as well, don't you think?

TBS: How does the kind of spaces available affect the kind of theatrical fare that is produced?

YB: London, where I have done most of my work over the years, leads the world in the imaginative use of what it calls found spaces. Warehouses, barns, drill halls, horticultural gardens and so on have all made enthralling theatre spaces. But the reliable provision of common or garden conventional theatres of all sizes and configurations is the key to honing the craft of both writers and practitioners of all skills – and never forgetting the appreciation of the audiences. So, to answer your question. In Jamaica, well Kingston anyway, we are extremely lucky to have such a variety of theatres in which to ply our craft. The Ward Theatre is a celebrated structure, a rare building in the hemisphere, which should be preserved at all costs even if it is to be moved brick by brick to say Hope Gardens or The Ranny Williams centre. At the School of Drama there is a fabulous theatre in the round, which most drama schools I know of would be very happy to have. The Creative Arts Centre also has two interesting venues that challenge the imagination and on Tom Redcam, the bevy of Little and Little Little to downright tiny sit in their car park. Kingston, of course, abounds in found theatre spaces like the Pantry and the Ex Drive-in. This is a lot of provision for a city of this size

TBS: Do you believe the Jamaican public has turned its back on itself by not investing more in theatrical spaces?

YB: I don't think we must even blame our audiences. Why should the ticket-purchasing public, which remains to my mind so loyal, bear criticism for what is perceived as lack of theatre spaces? It's the duty of those who earn their living from theatre to lobby, to invest, to pay their bills on time, to provide the safe venues for their work. They must make sure that public (read Government again) funds are available to subsidize their art and their creative endeavours. The paying public will always support them if they get it right.

INDEX

A Liberated Woman (Barry Reckord), 78, 81 n. 4

A Midsummer Night's Dream, 56, 57, 58

A Raisin in the Sun (Hansberry), 55

Abbensetts, Michael, 79, 80, 81 n. 5, 88

Against His Will (Heron), 80, 88, 92 n. 3, 104, 106

Albee, Edward, 16

Allen, Carolyn, 13

Anansi and Brer Englishman, 63

Anderson, Beverly, 53

Anderson, Clive, 105

Arawak Gold (Dwyer), 78

Ashbourne, Peter, 54, 57, 59 n. 2

Ask Your Mama (Hughes), 36, 37, 38, 77

Audiences and economic survival, 8, 105; marketing The Barn, 43

Ba, Miriama, 99

Back-o-the-Barn Ceramics, 44-45

Banana Boy (Hillary), 49

Bandoolu Version (Ford Smith), 95, 96

Banks, John, 45

Barrow, Lois Kelly, 22, 26 n. 10, 43

Bartley, Janet, 35, 40 n. 7, 54, 55, 56, 58

Batson Savage, Tanya, 126

Beal, Paul, 123

Bell, Christine, 77

Bell, Vera, 26 n. 14

Bell, Vera, 26 n. 14

Bellamy, Richille, 110

Bellas Gate Boy (Rhone), 18, 19, 25 n. 1, 33, 63, 71, 100

Bellywoman Bangarang (Sistren), 94, 95-96

Bennett, Louise, 22, 23, 26 n. 9, 27 n. 15, 43, 55, 67

Bennett, Melba, 36, 48, 49, 100

Bennett, Wycliffe, 14, 15 n. 4, 66, 87

Bethencourt, John, 111

Binns, Graham, 43, 49

Black, Neville, 49

Blake, Hope, 106

Body Moves (King), 91

Bradshaw, Carl, 61, 62, 101

Brady, Harold, 67

Breadfruit Kingdom (P. Brown), 106

Brecht, Bertolt, 55, 56

Brewster, Yvonne (see also Jones, Yvonne), 7, 8, 9, 10, 11, 12, 13, 56, 66, 127

Brodber, Andrew, 110

Brother Desmond (Denton), 122

Brown, Arthur, 77

Brown, Jonathan, 78

Brown, Lloyd, 111

Brown, Nicky, 71

Brown, Patrick, 80, 85, 86, 105, 106, 111, 124, 126

Bruckings (Dwyer), 78

Bullins, Ed, 46, 51 n. 8

Bully, Alwin, 30, 39 n. 3, 85, 87, 101, 111, 112

Burke, Sheila, 44

Buss Out (Cumper), 96

Butler, Calvin, 106

Calabash Literary Festival, 70, *Bellas Gate Boy* at, 71

Campbell, Glen, 67, 104, 106

Canton, Betty, 49

Carter, George, 24, 37, 41 n. 16, 48, 141

Carty, David, 102

Case, Roy, 48, 101, 102

Castro, Fidel, 107

Centre for Creative Arts, 21, 24, 30, 61, 79, 102, 118, 124, 142

Champagne and Sky Juice (Dawkins), 73 n.4, 86, 101

Channer, Colin, 70

Chippy (Hillary), 49, 51 n. 9, 117

Chuck, Valerie, 70, 121, 122, 124

Clarke, Claude (YB's father), 19, 29, 31, 33, 43

Clarke, Kathleen (YB's mother), 19, 31, 33, 43, 44, 51 n. 1

Clayton, Cecile, 78

Cole, Ken, 52

Comic Strip (Rhone), 62, 63, 72, 100, 101, 103

Commedia de'll arte, 64, 73-74, n. 6

Conrad, Joseph, 15

Cook, Tom, 52

Cooke, Aston, 80, 85, 106, 111, 123, 125

Cooke, Ruel, 77

Cooney, Ray, 106

Corbyn, Jeremy, 14

Cornflakes (Brown), 86, 105, 111

Corsbie, Ken, 113

Country Duppy (Cooke), 106

Couples (Dawkins), 80, 89, 123

Cousins, Frank, 63

Cowan, Pauline, 67, 78, 100

Creighton, Charmaine, 89

Cromwell, Ernest, 58

Crosskill, Darryl, 35, 47

Crosskill, Vaughn, 61, 101

Cumper, Pat, 62, 73 n. 5, 96

Daley-Salmon, Andrea, 100

Dark and Light Theatre, Brixton, 63

Dawes, Carroll, 10

Dawes, Kwame, 70, 86

Dawkins, Basil, 61, 72 n. 4, 80, 85, 89, 90, 91, 110, 111, **115-120**: memories of The Barn, 115, interview 116-120, 123, 124, 126, 129, 141

Days, Jessie, 39

Death Row (Daley-Salmon), 100

December (P. Brown), 106

Deloris (Bethencourt), 101, 102, 111

Dem Two, 75, 113

Denton, Michael, 122

Deportee Round 2 (Knight), 111

Derby, Vernon, 66, 67

Did Mama Know? (Beal), 123

Divorce Papers (Dawkins), 116

Dream on Monkey Mountain (Walcott), 40 n. 9

Drums and Colours (Walcott), 26 n. 6

Dwyer, Ted, 78

Ebanks, Roderick, 117

Economics and theatre, 8, 68; the writer/producer, 68, 86; Rhone as professional, 72; the commercial Jamaican theatre, 85-86, 107-108, 119; benefit performances, 120

Ecstasy (Heron), 92, 106

Edna Manley School of the Visual and Performing Arts, 30, 40 n. 3, 87

Electronic Nigger (Bullins), 46

Eliot, Bev Didi, 95

Ellington, Fae, 98, 101, 110

Emigration from Jamaica, 8; of the middle class, 107

Empire Road (Abbensetts), 79

Everyman (Rhone), 67, 72

Facey, Howard, 78

Flat Mate (Dawkins), 89

Forbes, Leonie, 16, 22, 26 n. 11, 43, 100, 101, 110

Ford Smith, Honor, 13, 73, 78, 79, 94, 95, 98 n. 2

Foreign Mind (Harrison), 106

Foster, Calvin, 67

Fowler, Henry and Greta, 24, 27 n. 17, 34, 54, 55, 93

Friends (P. Brown), 86, 106

Front Room (Cooke), 106

Fuller, Maude, 65

Garbutt, Andrew, 31, 32, 34, 54, 58

Gilkes, Michael, 113, 114 n. 7

Gloudon, Ancile, 60, 73 n.1

Gloudon, Barbara, 23, 27 n. 16, 51 n. 2, 52, 93

Go Tell it on Table Mountain (Evan Jones), 55, 56, 57

Gonzales, Christopher, 45, 51 n. 6

Greasy Spoon (King), 86, 89, 91

Green Pastures (Marc Connolly), 25

Guava Jelly (P. Brown), 106

Hansberry, Lorraine, 55

Harris, Dahlia, 93, 98 n.1

Harrison, Stafford (Ashani), 75, 76, 77, 78, 79, 81 n. 1, 86, 105, 106, 126, 141

Hart, Joanna, 35, 50, 54, 57, 58 n. 2

Hart, Karl, 25

Heap, Brian, 67, 87

Hearne, Anna, 76
Hearne, John, 31, 39, 41 n. 11, 141
Henry, Edward, 76
Henry, Zac, 78
Henzell, Justine, 70
Heron, David, 80, 86, 88, 92 n. 3, 106
Hibbert, Sydney, 16, 17, 18, 31, 32, 34, 126, 127, 130 n. 1
Hickling, Freddie, 96, 102
Hill, Raymond, 49
Hill, Robert, 46, 47
Hillary, Sam, 33, 49, 50, 51 n. 9, 117
Hitchens, Pam (Mordecai), 31, 34, 40 n. 5
Ho Shing, Ruth, 100
Hoilett, Pablo, 25, 27 n. 21, 80, 92, 101, 102, 110
Hopkinson, Slade (Abdhur Rahman), 36, 41 n. 15, 101
Hot Flashes (Raskin et al), 100, 101
How's the World Treating You (Milner), 21, 31, 33
Hughes, Langston, 35, 37, 38, 77
Hunt, Denise, 110
Hyatt, Charles, 69, 102, 103, 104, 110
I'm Human, Right (Binns), 49
Ione (Walcott), 118
Irons, Aggrey, 79
Irons, Stan, 48, 61, 101
It's Not My Fault, Baby (Rhone, Crosskill, Martin), 47, 48, 100
Jack and the Beanstalk, 23
Jam Biz, 106, 121
Jamaica2Rahtid (Cooke), 106, 123, 125
Jamaica Rundown (Cooke), 80
Jamaican education in *School's Out*, 64-66
Jamaican theatre before independence, 8
James, C.L.R., 107
Johnson, Bari, 101, 102
Johnson, Volier, 32, 58 n. 1
Jones, Evan, 55, 57
Jones, Leroi (Amiri Baraka), 47
Jones, Ray, 46
Jones, Yvonne (Brewster), 17, 31, 32, 38, 49, 56, 66, 127

Joyce, Elizabeth, 50
Kerr, Bobb, 67, 101, 122
Killa Sound (Harrison), 86
Killer (King), 86, 89
Kincaid, Jamaica, 99
King, Hugh, 85, 86, 89, 90- 92, 111, 115
Kiss Mi Neck (Cooke), 106
Knight, Ginger, 61, 73 n.2, 111, 120, 123
Koo Koo (Hillary), 34, 49, 50
Labour Ward (P. Brown), 111
Ladies of the Night (Brown), 106
Lannaman, Grace, 16, 17, 18, 31, 32, 34, 127
Lee, Easton, 33, 116, 117, 120 n. 1
Leslie, Marcia, 100, 110
Lewin, Olive, 55, 56, 95
Lewis, Bim, 54, 57, 58, 59 n. 4
Lindsay, Hertencer, 96, 100
Lindsay, Pat, 78
Little Theatre Movement (LTM), 24
Little-White, Lennie, 39, 42 n. 21
Lockhart, Calvin, 47
Look Two (Rhone), 39, 45, 60
Mais, Roger, 36, 39, 42 n. 20
Malcolm, Dervan, 110
Manley, Douglas, 38
Manley, Edna, 44, 51 n. 3
Manley, Michael, 52, 53, 61, 106, 107, 108, 118
Manley, Rachel, 65, 74 n. 9
Marriott, Louis, 69, 80, 105, 123, 125
Martin, Jackson (alias of Sonia Mills), 35, 36, 100
Masqueraders (Harrison), 79, 81
Matthews, Marc, 75, 113
Maxwell, Ken, 52
Maxwell, Marina, 24, 27 n. 20
McCalla, Barbara, 100, 101, 109
McFarlane, Basil, 36, 41 n. 12
McFarlane, J.E.C., 36
McFarlane, Pearl, 110
McGhie, Grace (Brown), 61, 62, 78, 98; interview **101-103**, 127
McKie, Vincent, 31, 32, 34, 50, 67

Meeks, Amina Blackwood, 110
Memory and writing the book, 14-15,
    loss of archives, 14
Methuen, Paul, 22, 43
Milner, Roger, 21, 26 n. 7
Mirro, Mirro (Sistren), 96, 97, 98
Miss Girlie, *84*
Miss Julie (Strindberg), 16
Morris, Mervyn, 26 n. 9, 36, 41 n. 13,
    58, 91, 141
Morris, Val, 78
Morrison, Glen, 61, 101
Mr. Drummond, 22
Murray, Gladstone, 76, 82, 83, 121, 122
Murray, Rosemary, 106
Music Boy (Rhone), 72
Muttoo, Henry, 113
Nairne, Trevor, 67, 70, 78, 80, 84, **85-
    92**, 96, 102, 105, 106, 109, 121,
    127, 129
Nana Ya (Sistren), 96
Neighbours (Saunders), 47
Nettleford, Rex, 49, 55
Nicholson, Hilary, 29, 76, 79, 96
Nicholson, Michael, 106
Night Work (King), 86, 89, 91, 92, 115
Nite Box (Bully), 40, 111
Noel, Keith, 87, 102, 105, 111
Office Chase (Marriott), 74 n. 14
Okri, Ben, 14
Old Dramatic Theatre, 24
Old Story Time (Rhone), 60, 63, 70,
    74 n. 11, 123
"On the Off Beat", 36, 37
One More Time (Simon), 110
One of Our Sons is Missing (Sealy), 110,
    113
One Stop Driver (Rhone & Marriott),
    63, 69, 80, 105
Orton, Joe, 58, 127
Osbourne, Kay, 29, 39 n. 1, 93, 94,
    100
Owen, Kathy, 110
Pantomime, Jamaicanising of British
    pantomime, 23, 26 n. 9, 10, 14,
    27 n. 16, 30, 34, 41 n. 16, 49, 55,
    58 n. 1, 63, 72, 76 n. 10, 78, 93,

98, 115, 128
Pantry Playhouse, 25
Parboosingh, Karl, 36, 38, 41 n. 14,
    46
Parchment, Trevor, 65
Parson and Mrs Jones (Dawkins), 73 n.
    4, 89, 111, 118
Part Time Lover (Knight), 73 n. 2, 123
Pastor Hoodini (Beal), 123
Pearson, Gene, 45
Peryer, Harvel, 62
Pinter, Harold, 50
Play It (Zacca), 80
Please (K. Maxwell), 52, 53
Porter, Eileen, 58
Porter, Jonathan, 58
Positive (Rhone), 63, 72
Postcolonial cultural drive, 7, 9, 10,
    85
Pouyatt, Buddy, 55, 56, 102
Power Play (Dawkins), 73, 110
Price, Teddy, 101, 110, 127
Priestley, J.B., 20
Priestley, Pat, 16, 17, 18, 31, 127
Professional theatre, the ambition, 8,
    12; returnees from UK and North
    American theatre training, 16
Puppy Love (P. Brown), 80, 86, 106
QPH (Sistren), 95
Race, class and colourism in Jamaican
    theatre, 23, 34, 47, 51 n. 1, 57
Rae, Norman, 87
Ramrod (King), 89, 91
Raskin, Barbara, 99
Reckord, Barry, 78, 108, 109, 112 n. 1
Reckord, Lloyd, 24, 27 n. 18, 79, 87,
    109, 110, 122
Reckord, Michael, 107, 113 n. 3, 122
Remembrance (Walcott), 87, 88, 127
Rhone, Jean, 110
Rhone, Neville, 52
Rhone, Trevor, 8, 10, 11, 13, 16, 17,
    18, 19, 25, 31, 32, 34, 35, 36, 38,
    40 n. 8, 47, 50, 51 n. 1, 54, 56, 58,
    60-74, 80, 86, 87, 90, 94, 96, 101,
    102, 105, 109, 110, 118, 120, 123,
    126, 127, 129-130, 141; on tourism,

64, on education, 64-66, on the feminine psyche, 68-69; as difficult collaborator, 69, 108

Rhys, Jean, 100

Robinson, Claudia, 100

Rodd, Ethlyn, 23

Rolando and Rosamund (Mais), 39

Roots theatre, 8, 30, 73 n. 2, 107, 108 n. 1, 122, 129

Rose Bruford Training College of Speech and Drama, 19, 28, 32, 35, 80

Royal Academy of Dramatic Art (London), 16

Rubin, Lillian, 100

Run for your Wife (Harrison/ adapted from Clooney), 105

Ryman, Cheryl, 36, 38, 39, 41 n.8, 48, 49, 141

Sala (Hopkinson), 36, 41, 63, 101, 102

Salmon, Kenny, 106

Salmon, Lenford, 105, 121

Samuels, Oliver, 55, 56, 66-67, 74 n. 12

Saunders, James, 47

Saving Alligator High (Brown), 106

School's Out (Rhone), 34, 63, 64, 66, 67, 68, 69, 72, 76, 100, 106

Scott, Alwyn, 71, 74 n. 15, 111, 115

Scott, Dawn, 45, 51 n. 7

Scott, Dennis, 33, 35, 36, 37, 39, 41 n 10, 45, 66, 72, 78, 87, 101, 102, 109, 129, 141

Sea at Dauphin (Walcott), 21

Sealy, Godfrey, 110, 113 n. 2

See Mama (Henry), 76

Shakespeare, William, 10, 22, 32, 34, 54, 57, 68, 91, 107, 118

Silvera, George, 44, 76, 84

Simon, Neil, 110

Single Entry (Cooke), 106

Sistren, 94, 95-96, 97, 98, 100, 141

Skeen, Paul, 110

Sleeper (Rhone), 36, 62, 63, 72, 101, 101

Small, Jean, **97-98**, 98 n. 3, 100, 101, 110

Smile Orange (Rhone), 36, 60, 61-64, 66, 67, 68, 70, 72, 75, 82, 101, 102, 103, 104, 115, 118, 123

Smith, Auriol (wife of Sam Walters), 54, 55

Smith, Penny (on roots theatre), 107-108

Soliday and the Wicked Bird (Bell), 23

Soyinka, Wole, 10, 107

Spence, Tricia, 110

Starting Over (King), 89, 91, 111

Straight Man (Tipling), 77, 79, 94, 100

Strindberg, August, 16, 126

Stuart, Cheryl, 62

Sugar D (B. Reckord), 110

Sutherland, Efua, 7

Sweet Talk (Abbensetts), 79, 80, 89

Taffe, Joe, 118

Talawa Theatre Company, 56, 62, 73 n. 5, 128

Tallawah online, 25, 123

Taylor, Jean, 45, 51 n. 5.

The Barn: its birth, 2, 22; naming and fitting it out, 28-30, 3, 44; physical intimacy of performance, 8, 30, 56; children's drama classes, 44, 51 n 2; marketing The Barn, 43; Munair Zacca in charge, 75-81; Gladstone Murray as caretaker and accountant, 82-84; Trevor Nairne in charge, 85-92; directors at the Barn, 109-114: Dennis Scott, 109, Lloyd Reckord, 109-110, Pablo Hoilett, 110-111, Ed Wallace, 111, Keith Noel, 111, Alwin Bully, 111; market forces and economic struggles, 122; physical deterioration and difficulty of funding rehabilitation, 122 harassment by licensing authorities and reduction in seats, 124; decision to sell the site, 126; physical disappearance, 11, 126; successes and failures, 127-129

The Collection (Pinter), 50

The Creatures (Waite-Smith), 21, 26 n.4

The Criminals (Triana), 76

The Father (Strindberg), 126

The Gadget (Rhone), 60, 63, 70, 72
The Game (Rhone), 8, 9, 63, 80
The Garden Theatre, 22, 43
The Harder They Come (film), 40 n. 7, 55, 58 n. 1, 62, 102
The Inquisitors (Scott), 36, 39
The Little Little Theatre, 25, 119, 124
The Little Theatre, 23-24, 26 n. 6, 30, 32, 37, 54, 55, 56, 72, 93, 120
The Quickie (Harrison), 79, 107
The Resurrection of Jonathan Digby (King), 89, 91
The Skeleton Inside (Tipling), 36, 77, 78, 81, 94, 100, 115
The Ward Theatre, 22-23, 26 n. 12, 30, 32, 98, 129, 134
Theatre 77, the goals, 16-17; problems of rehearsal space, 17, 31; financial fiasco of first performance and fallings-out of group, 18, 33, 48; devising plays through improvisation, 35; problems of finding Jamaican work, 46; plays that did not speak to the local audience, 50; criticism in local media, 52; offending Michael Manley, 53; taking Shakespeare to schools, 54, 56, 57-58; theatre visitors from the UK; Sam Walters, 54-57, the Porters, 58; the stream of plays from Trevor Rhone, 60-73; YB's departure for the UK, 1971, 62, return in 1974.
Theatre Place, 25
Thomas, Eddie, 55
Thomas, Fabian, 72
Thomas, Tess, 48
Thompson, Natalie, 87, 102
Time and the Conways (J.B. Priestley), 20
Tipling, Carmen, 36, 77, 81 n. 3, 91, 94, 100, 115, 127, 141
Tjon, Henk, 101, 102, 109
Tomlin, Joshua, 122
Tourism, in *Smile Orange*, 64
Toy Boy (Dawkins), 73
Trial of One Short-Sighted Black Woman (Leslie), 100, 110

Triana, Jose, 76, 81 n. 2
Tucker, Winston, 105
Under Mi Nose 3 (Beal), 123
Undercover Lover (King), 86, 91
Underwriters Under Cover (Knight), 73 n. 2, 123
Vaz, Noel, 21, 26 n. 6
Waite-Smith, Cecily, 21
Walcott, Derek, 10, 21, 26 n. 6, 40 n. 9, 87, 88, 108, 127
Wallace, Ed, 58, 101, 111
Walters, Sam, 34, 40 n. 6; on stay in Jamaica and at The Barn, 54-56, 57
Warner Bros., 77, 81, 100
Warner, Earl, 110
Way Out Theatre, 25
Weller, Del, 37
Western aesthetics and Jamaican sensibility, 8
What the Butler Saw (Orton), 34, 58, 99, 127
When the Cat's Away (Hoilett), 111
Whylie, Marjorie, 65, 74 n. 10, 101
Williams, Eugene, 30, 40 n. 4, 87
Williams, Ranny, 23, 27 n. 15, 55
Wilson, Gladstone, 49
Wipe That Smile (Osbourne), 29, 93-94, 100
Workshop Theatre Trinidad (Walcott), 10
Woung, Billy, 16, 17, 18, 31, 32, 127
Xperiment, 39
Yard 89, 90 (P. Brown), 106
Yard Theatre (Marina Maxwell), 24, 27 n. 20
Yes Mama (Rhone), 49, 60, 68
You in Your Small Corner (B. Reckord), 109
Zacca, Munair, 16, 17, 18, 19, 22, 31, 32, 35, 36, 38, 39, 40 n. 9, 43, 47, 48, 49, 50, 52, 54, 56, 57, 58, 67, 72, **76-81**, 82,, 84, 87, 88, 105, 112, 113, 127, 129
Zinn, Phillip, 52
Zoo Story (Albee), 16

Born in Kingston, Jamaica, Yvonne Brewster went to the UK to study drama in the mid-1950s at the Rose Bruford College – where she was the UK's first Black woman drama student – and at the Royal Academy of Music, where she received a distinction in Drama and Mime, and was a pupil of Marcel Marceau. She returned to Jamaica to teach Drama and in 1965 she also jointly founded (with Trevor Rhone) The Barn in Kingston, Jamaica's first professional theatre company.

Upon her return to England she worked extensively in radio, television, and directing for Stage Productions. She has worked on many films, among them *The Harder They Come, Smile Orange* and *The Marijuana Affair*, and for BBC TV *The Fight Against Slavery* and *My Father Sun Sun Johnson*. Between 1982 and 1984, she was Drama Officer at the Arts Council of Great Britain. Revered as one of Britain's best established and most respected black theatre directors, Yvonne was until February 2003 Artistic Director of the country's leading black theatre company, Talawa, which she established in 1985 together with Mona Hammond, Inigo Espegel and Carmen Munroe.

She was awarded an Order of the British Empire for Services to the Arts in 1993, and in 2001 she was granted an honorary Doctorate from the Open University. In 2005, the University of London's Central School of Speech and Drama conferred an honorary fellowship on Brewster in acknowledgment of her involvement in the development of British theatre.

In 2004 she published *The Undertaker's Daughter: The Colourful Life of a Theatre Director* (Arcadia Books). She has also edited five collections of plays, including Barry Reckord's *For the Reckord* (Oberon Books, 2010) and *Mixed Company: Three Early Jamaican Plays*, published by Oberon Books in 2012.

OTHER BOOKS ON CARIBBEAN THEATRE

Olivier Stephens
Visions and Voices
ISBN: 9781845231736; pp. 436; pub. 2013; price £19.99.

In the 1970s and 1980s Olivier Stephenson was very actively engaged in Caribbean theatre in New York. There he met a number of Caribbean playwrights, either already living there or making visits. He was looking for plays, they for theatres and performers. Out of this connection came this hugely important and unrepeatable collection of fourteen interviews with most of the founding figures of contemporary Anglophone Caribbean theatre. As the preface by Kwame Dawes indicates, the period of the interviews, from the mid 1970s into the 1980s, was a crucial one for the Caribbean theatre, as its most productive and revolutionary period, and a time when it was already taking on the variety of forms and locations that still characterise it today.

Besides talking about their own influences, experiences, goals and aesthetic visions, each playwright contributes to a collective picture of Caribbean theatre being defined by its spaces – diasporic or regional, proscenium or open air; the nature of its audiences – a heated debate about the possibilities for a commercial theatre that has the work of Trevor Rhone at its heart – and the playwright's relationship to inherited theatre traditions and to specifically Caribbean cultural resources. Reflective, analytical, visionary, opinionated – these are lively interviews, not least because Olivier Stephenson asked each of the playwrights for their views on their peers – views sometimes given with acerbic frankness.

This collection should, of course, have been published many years ago, and the subsequent deaths of eight of the interviewees make it something of a memorial, but the interviews themselves read as freshly as when they were recorded. With extensive annotations and end notes, and insightful introductions by Kwame Dawes and Olivier Stephenson, this is an essential book for anyone interested in contemporary Caribbean theatre and its history.

Interviews: Derek Walcott, Errol Hill, Errol John, Michael Abbensetts, Trevor Rhone, Alwyn Bully, Roderick Walcott, Edgar White, Slade Hopkinson, Lennox Brown, Carmen Tipling, Dennis Scott, Stafford Ashani Harrison, Mustapha Matura .

Patricia Cumper
Inner Yardie: Three Plays
ISBN: 9781845232320; pp. 196; pub. 2014; price £9.99

Patricia Cumper writes that the motivation for each of the plays in this collection was anger. *The Rapist*, which ran for six months in Jamaica, does indeed involve a rapist who insinuates himself into the trust of the main character, but the fury inside the play is as much concerned with the repressive dynamics of a respectable middle-class family as it is to do with a specific act of misogynist violence. With lines that challenge the audience to laughter, and then to question why they are laughing, this is a powerful piece of theatre about gender and class.

The impetus to take on Romeo and Juliet in *Benny's Song* was no less to do with fury – with the political violence destroying the lives of so many young people in Jamaica in the 1980s. In the nation-language of the streets, *Benny's Song* adapts the narrative of star-crossed love to the tragic mix of ideology, communalism, criminality and the tempting erotics of violence in the ghettos of Kingston.

The Key Game is set in a rundown psychiatric hospital in Jamaica that the government is demolishing to make way for some profitable real estate. The three remaining inmates and their nurse, Norman, are in a state of panic about their imminent release. But this is not really a play about care in the community. What Dappo, Gonzalez, Shakespeare and Norman (characters that Samuel Beckett might have been pleased to own) must confront are issues of a far more existential kind.

With introductory essays by the author and Kwame Dawes, these plays confirm Patricia Cumper as one of the most original and challenging of Caribbean and Black British playwrights.